THE SECRET SOLDIER

★ ★ ★ ★ ★ ★ ★ ★ ★ ★ ★ ★ ★ ★ ★ ★ ★ ★ ★ ★

The Story of Deborah Sampson

By Ann McGovern

Illustrated by Harold Goodwin
Cover illustration by Katherine Thompson

ISBN 0-590-43052-1

5 6 7/0

40

SCHOLASTIC INC.
New York Toronto London Auckland Sydney

Sent Away

Deborah's mother looked down at her five sleeping children. She had not slept all night.

In a few hours the sun would come up. It would be a new day — the terrible day she would have to give her children away.

Deborah's father had left home to sail the seas in search of adventure. Now he was dead, drowned in a shipwreck at sea.

Deborah's mother was sick and poor. She could no longer take care of all her little ones.

She touched the sleeping children, one by one. Her hand stayed the longest on Deborah's soft, brown hair.

"You are most like your father," she thought. "It is you I will miss the most."

Deborah Sampson was only five years old when she had to leave her mother and her home in Plympton, Massachusetts. It was the year 1765, ten years before the start of the Revolutionary War.

She was sent to live with Miss Fuller, her mother's cousin.

Cousin Fuller was sweet and jolly. She never had children of her own. But she knew just what would make a sad little girl happy again.

She baked cookies for Deborah. She gave Deborah a bed of her own — a soft feather bed that she did not have to share with anyone.

Deborah loved her kind cousin.

Miss Fuller taught her how to spin and weave, and how to make bread.

But best of all were the wonderful hours of reading lessons.

Deborah learned the alphabet by heart. She learned to read quickly.

For three years Deborah was happy.

Then one day Miss Fuller became ill. Three days later she was dead. Deborah cried. Dear, sweet Cousin Fuller. She had been like a mother to Deborah.

Deborah was now eight years old and without a home. Her own mother was still too sick to take care of her. She tried to find another place for Deborah to live.

The only person who would take Deborah in was 80-year-old Mrs. Thatcher, who lived in Middleborough.

Mrs. Thatcher must be the oldest lady in the world, Deborah thought.

Mrs. Thatcher was too feeble to do anything for herself. Deborah had to do everything. She had to feed old Mrs. Thatcher like a baby. The old lady could hardly lift her spoon to her mouth.

Deborah did all the hard work too. She carried in heavy loads of wood for the fire. She kept the fire going and swept up the ashes. She washed the clothes and did all of the cooking.

Every day was like every other — full of hard work and loneliness.

It was too much for an eight-year-old girl.

But there was nothing else Deborah could do. That's how it was for a poor girl without anyone to take care of her.

"If only I could see my mother," Deborah thought over and over.

But her mother lived too far away and besides, who would take Deborah there?

Sometimes Deborah thought she did not have a friend in all the world.

She was wrong.

The minister of Middleborough thought about Deborah often. He came to see how she was getting on.

He saw the feeble old lady nodding her head by the fire. He saw Deborah growing taller — and thinner — and paler.

The good minister made a promise to himself. "I will get this child out of here," he said.

He kept his promise.

Mrs. Thatcher was sent to live with relatives. And Deborah was sent to live with Deacon Thomas and his family in the same town of Middleborough.

A Family Again

A family! A laughing, loving, crying, hugging family! Deborah had almost forgotten what a family was.

But the Thomas family was not *her* family. She knew what she was in the Thomas household. A servant. And she knew she would have to be a servant for 10 years. That was the agreement. Deacon Thomas would give her a place to stay, food to eat, and clothes to wear. Deborah knew she would have to work hard for 10 years.

Ten years. A long time.

"What will I be like in 10 years?" she wondered. Ten years from now was too far away to think about. Better think about right now. At least she had her own little room, above the kitchen, in the loft upstairs.

And there was plenty to do right now. Mrs. Thomas had four lively little boys for her to look after. She dressed the youngest, fed them, and told them stories. She helped with every job in the house and in the barn. She swept, cleaned, cooked, carried in the wood, and brought in the water.

But the family was so lively and Deborah was kept so busy that she soon forgot the lonely, long days at Mrs. Thatcher's house.

There was so much to do, Deborah hardly had a moment to herself. She had no time to do what she liked best — reading.

In those days, people did not think it was important for girls to read. Some people thought too much reading gave girls brain fever.

Deacon Thomas and his wife thought all a girl had to learn was how to work well.

Deborah was a good worker. She grew strong as she milked the cows, fed the pigs, and tended the chickens. She learned how to harness the family horse, and she rode the horse to the village on errands.

She helped plow the fields. When it looked like rain, she raked up all the hay and stored it neatly inside the barn. She learned how to make the things she needed — a basket, a sled, a milking stool.

Deborah taught the three oldest boys how to read. So when summer came, they were ready to go to the summer school in the village.

School started at 6:30 in the morning and lasted two and half hours. Then the boys came home to do their share of work. Late in the afternoon they went back to school.

Deborah would stand at the window and watch the boys run laughing down the road.

"If only I could go with them," she thought.

When the boys came home, she begged them to teach her what they had learned that day. But they didn't want to talk about school or learning. They only wanted to wrestle with her and tease her.

The Thomas children thought Deborah was odd, even a little crazy. Why did she care so much about school? Why did she ask so many questions?

How do flowers and vegetables grow, and why?

What are the stars made of? How far away are they?

What makes the sun set and the moon rise?

Deborah often got up before the sun rose and climbed to the top of a nearby hill to watch the night sky lighten into day.

Deborah begged Deacon Thomas to let her go to school sometimes. But there was always too much work to do.

There was a new baby in the house now and another on the way. She couldn't be spared.

So Deborah borrowed the children's school books. At night, in her little room above the kitchen, she read until her candle flickered out.

She practiced writing with a pen she made herself from goose feathers. She dipped the pen into homemade ink and wrote on a piece of bark from a birch tree.

She started writing in a diary — a book in which she wrote down her good and her bad thoughts and deeds.

On the right-hand pages she wrote down all of her good thoughts and the good things she had done.

On the left-hand pages she wrote down all the things she thought of as bad. The left-hand pages filled up first.

Deacon Thomas had to say to her often, "I wish you wouldn't spend so much time scribbling."

There was one lesson Deacon Thomas thought all his children should learn — how to use money wisely. Every child in the family was given some lambs to raise and sell. They were allowed to keep the money to buy something useful.

Deacon Thomas let Deborah have some lambs too. She took good care of her flock and got a good price for them.

It was the first time she ever had money of her own. She had earned it herself. It was a good feeling. Carefully, she wrapped the money in a handkerchief and put it away.

A Country in Trouble

The America of Deborah Sampson's time was nothing like the America of today, with its millions of people living in 50 states.

Most of the country was still wilderness, where Indians lived.

People had come from across the ocean and settled in colonies along the Eastern coast. Deborah was born in the Massachusetts Bay Colony. There were 13 colonies. Most of the people who settled there were English and all of the

13 colonies belonged to England. The people were ruled by the King of England far across the sea.

In time, many people in the 13 colonies wanted to be free from English rule. They wanted to make their own laws.

But the King of England wanted to keep his colonies. He needed money for his government. One way to get money from the colonies was to make the people pay taxes.

Most of the people in the colonies did not think that was fair. The King made rules about many things the people did not think were fair — rules about hunting and farming and fishing. Rules about running their business and even rules about worshipping God.

Year after year, the trouble between the colonies and England got worse.

In every village, on every farm, the people talked about the troubles.

Should America be free from England? they asked. Even if it meant war?

Like everyone else, Deborah Sampson heard about the troubles too.

1770 Deborah was 10 years old.

In Boston, the people were angry. The King of England had sent over his red-coated soldiers to see that his rules were carried out. The Americans didn't want the soldiers there in the first place. And then they heard they would have to pay for the soldiers' expenses.

1773 Deborah was 13 years old.

Although most Americans loved to drink tea, they said they would not buy all their tea from England. They wanted to be free to buy tea from any country they chose.

But England sent over ships loaded with tea anyway. One night in Boston, some Americans dressed up as Indians.

They went aboard the three English ships in the harbor and they dumped all that tea into the water.

Deborah heard about the Boston Tea Party, and laughed. But when the English King heard about it, he was furious. He sent over more red-coated soldiers.

1774 Deborah was 14 years old.

The King punished the people of Boston. He said no ships could sail in or out of Boston until the tea was paid for.

Everyone worried that the people of Boston would starve. They thought of ways to help them. Some people planted extra corn to send to the hungry people of Boston. Deborah helped plant the corn on the Thomas farm.

1775   Deborah was 15.

The trouble was getting worse. In many villages, people were getting ready for war. Groups of men and young boys began training to be soldiers. They were called minutemen because they were ready to fight at a minute's notice.

Deborah watched them drill in her village.

People in many villages began to collect guns and barrels of powder. They hid them in secret places.

One night, the British soldiers were sent to the town of Concord, near Boston, to seize the hidden guns and powder.

But some colonists found out where the British soldiers were going. The people had to be warned! The minutemen had to be called out!

That night Paul Revere and William Dawes rode their horses on the roads to Lexington and Concord, warning the people, "The British are coming."

So by the time the British soldiers reached the town of Lexington, near Concord, they found more than 50 minutemen ready for them.

The fight that followed was the first of the Revolutionary War.

Deborah heard the bells of Middleborough ringing, marking that first battle of the long war ahead.

1776 Deborah was 16.

A brave farmer from Virginia had been chosen to lead the American army. His name was George Washington.

In the city of Philadelphia, an important paper was being read before the first Congress. That paper was the Declaration of Independence. It said that all men were created equal. And it said that they have the right to form their own government, to be a free country — free from England's rule.

On July 4, 1776, the people in Congress voted for the Declaration of Independence — they voted to be the United States of America. News of the new government reached across the land. Deborah heard the bells of Middleborough ring out again.

But not everyone in the colonies wanted the new United States. Some people still wanted to belong to England. They were still loyal to the English king. These people were called *Tories*.

It was one thing for America to say it was free. But it was another thing to win freedom!

1778 Deborah was 18.

The war was long. The news was sad. So many times it seemed that the United States was losing the war.

Then help came from France. Ships and soldiers came from France to help the weary American soldiers.

France helped America win some of the important battles that would put an end to the long, long war.

The Thomas children were growing up. Deborah said good-bye to the oldest boy who left home and went to war.

Free - to Do What?

Year by year, the United States was growing closer to the time when it could stand alone.

And year by year, Deborah was growing closer to her independence too — the time she could go out into the world and be on her own.

At last Deborah was 18 years old. It was the year 1778 and she was free!

But free to do what? She was a woman. That meant she could not learn a trade, the way young men did.

The Thomas family still needed Deborah's help around the house and farm. They asked her to stay on for the winter.

It was her first winter of freedom, but she spent it doing the same kind of work she had done for the past ten years.

In the summertime she left the Thomas house.

She was going to be a schoolteacher! She—Deborah Sampson—who had never even been to school as a pupil was going to teach in the town school.

It was because of the war. Every man who could have taught in the summer school was busy with the war. There was no one left to teach.

Some people knew that Deborah had taught reading and writing to the Thomas children.

She might work out, they thought.

Hope and fear were all mixed up in Deborah when she left the Thomas house. She took a room in the house next door to the school in the village.

The school was the same as other schools of New England. There were a few books — the *New England Primer* and a spelling book and a few bibles.

There were a few girls in her class of 20 pupils. She remembered how she would have given almost anything to be able to go to school and learn when she

was young. So although she was supposed to teach the girls only sewing and knitting, and how to read a little, she taught them everything she knew. She taught them spelling and writing and everything she had read about stars and rivers and mountains.

How proud she was at the end of the summer when she was asked to come back the next year.

But what could she do all those months until next summer came?

Maybe her mother would have an idea. Deborah went to visit her.

Deborah's mother worried about her.

"Why aren't you thinking about getting married, child, like girls are supposed to do?" her mother asked.

In those days girls were expected to get married as soon as they could. Then they were expected to begin to raise a big family.

Deborah loved children, but she wanted

San Francisco Public Library
Due Date Receipt

Library Loc.: Bernal Heights
01/08/2022

Item(s) checked out to 21223....593.

1. The secret soldier : the story of
Barcode: 333410070405039alfr
Due Date: 01-29-22

Thank you for visiting the library!
Visit us at online at sfpl.org.

Questions? Email info@sfpl.org or call
415-557-4400.

to do other things — daring things — before she married and settled down.

In those days, married women had very few rights. A married woman could not have a house or a farm or money of her own. The law said everything she had belonged to her husband. She could not own anything. The husband had the right to make the decisions about everything — even what happened to the children.

No, Deborah was in no hurry to get married.

Deborah dreamed of a great adventure. Doing housework from morning till night and looking after a house full of babies was not her idea of a great adventure. Not yet. Not now.

Now she wanted to travel, to walk in different places, to see different faces.

During the war she had heard of Boston, Philadelphia, New York. Would she ever see those great cities?

In those days, if a poor man wanted to travel and have adventures, he joined the army.

"Why can't I join the army too?" Deborah thought. Then she laughed at herself.

"Me — Deborah Sampson — a soldier!" she thought. She knew the army was only for men.

"Wait," she told herself. "Why not me? Wasn't I a teacher without ever going to school? Wasn't I a *good* teacher?

Why not a soldier? Why not dress like a man and be a soldier!"

She went to sleep that night thinking about it. She dreamed about it.

And when she woke up, her head was filled with the single thought. It wasn't a dream now. It was a hope — a plan — a secret plan!

That winter she worked as a weaver. She lived in one home for weeks at a time while she wove clothes for the family. Then she moved on to another home.

She was weaving cloth, but she was also weaving plans. She told no one about them. There was no one to share her secret with, no one to give her advice.

Her plans grew sharper in her mind.

She had some money, wrapped in a handkerchief, that first money she had earned from selling her sheep long ago.

But she would need more money. She would have to get new clothes — men's clothes.

The Fortune Teller

When Deborah was 21, the Americans won an important battle at Yorktown, Virginia. But the fighting was not yet over.

America had a big problem with Tories. Tories were people who lived in America but who believed America should still be ruled by England. Tories did not want America to be a free and independent country.

Often the Tories would steal food and guns from the Americans and give them to the British soldiers. Often the Tories and the Americans fought each other.

By now the people were getting tired of fighting. The war had been dragging on for six years.

General Washington began calling for a different kind of soldier. He did not want the old kind of fighting men — the men who would stay in the army for only a few months and then go back to their farms.

He wanted soldiers to sign up for the army for three years at a time. Continental soldiers, they were called.

Many men were answering the call and signing up for three years.

Deborah was getting more and more restless.

She would do one more weaving job.

She wove cloth to tie around her chest so she would look flat-chested, like a boy. She wove a piece of cloth big enough to make a man's suit of clothes for herself. She bought a man's hat and shoes.

One day she put on all her clothes for the first time.

"Do I still look like me?" she wondered. "Would my mother know me?"

She would make another trip to her mother. It would be a test!

She passed it. Her own mother did not know her.

A fortune-teller lived near her mother's house. Deborah, wearing her man's disguise, went to see him.

"I am not here to take your advice," she said in the deepest voice she could manage. "I am only curious as to what you will say to me."

"You are an honest man," the fortune-teller told Deborah. "I see in your future many adventures. But not all of them will be successful."

Deborah's Secret Plan

Deborah's mind was made up. She would go to Boston and enlist in the army.

But she would wait a while longer. The weather in March was cold and stormy. She would have to travel alone through deep snows and in winds that could knock her down.

She would wait for spring.

Deborah used her free time getting used to acting like a man. When no one was looking, she put on her strange clothes. She practiced sitting and standing and walking and running and speaking in a deep voice.

The weather became warmer. The melting snows dripped down from the great pine trees. Birds sang, and a young man fell in love with Deborah.

Deborah's mother could not see why her daughter did not like him.

"He is a lump of a man," Deborah told her mother. "That's why."

One day he came to see Deborah. He was drunk. He had been drinking too much rum. Deborah wrote in her diary: "From that day on, I set him down a fool."

Deborah was ready to set her secret plan into action.

She went to bed at her regular bedtime. She slept for a few hours and woke at midnight. Deborah put on her man's clothes. She set off for the town of Taunton, 10 miles away. She walked all night. The next morning she saw her old neighbor, William Bennett, walking toward her. Her eyes met his and she jumped. Did he know her? Her heart pounded like a drum. Could he hear it? Surely she would be followed, she thought.

She made for the woods. She sat under a big pine tree. She had been walking for such a long time. She was so tired. Soon she was fast asleep.

It was dark when she woke up. Where was the road? At last she found it. Again she walked all night. She walked and she walked — and she found herself back in her old neighborhood!

"Give up!" one part of her cried. "You can't do it. Stay home where you belong!"

"Go on!" another part of her cried. "You can do it. Think of the adventures. You want to see rivers and mountains and cities. You want to see Boston."

She went on to Boston, walking all the way.

Deborah thought Boston must be the biggest city in the world. She had never seen that many people before in one place. Or that many houses. Or streets. Or horses and carriages. Or soldiers. . .

Deborah was hungry. She didn't have any money left, not even a penny for bread. It was time for the next part of her plan.

They Call Her "Bobby"

On May 20, 1782, Deborah Sampson joined the army as a Continental soldier. She said her name was Robert Shurtliff.

"We'll put you down for three years, if the war lasts that long," she was told as she signed her strange new name.

At first she was afraid to open her mouth to speak, afraid that she could not keep her voice deep enough.

At first she was afraid someone would find out she was a woman by the way she sat or walked or shook hands.

But wonder of wonders — no one guessed who she really was!

They thought she was young — 15 years old — because she had no beard. Most of the time the men called her Bobby. But sometimes, to tease her, they called her "Blooming Boy."

Her first test as a soldier was a hard one. She had to make a long march to West Point in New York.

She marched with 50 men. The march took almost two weeks. Every day she grew more and more tired, until she felt she could not go on. Every night she fell asleep in her clothes, like the rest of the soldiers.

One chilly, rainy afternoon the soldiers stopped to rest at a tavern. Deborah was warming herself at the fireplace. Suddenly she fainted and fell to the floor.

When she came to, her first thought was: "Have I been discovered?" Then she heard someone say, "What a pity such a young boy has to go to war."

Deborah breathed a sigh of relief. Her secret was still safe.

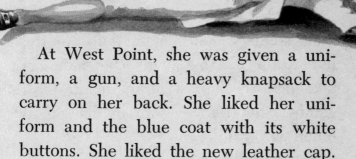

At West Point, she was given a uniform, a gun, and a heavy knapsack to carry on her back. She liked her uniform and the blue coat with its white buttons. She liked the new leather cap.

Every day she had to clean her gun and take part in the daily drill. She went on many raids against Tories. Soon she stopped thinking of war as an adventure.

War was the most horrible thing in the world, she thought. She heard the cries of men in pain. She saw them being shot down. She watched them die.

She had to go on long, long marches. Her shoes fell apart. Often she had to go without food for days. Sometimes she got so many blisters and sores on her hands she could hardly open or close her fingers.

But she never complained, and the other soldiers liked her for that. She did not drink or sing with the men, or take part in their wrestling contests or games. She tried to stay by herself as much as possible.

Everyone liked her. No one suspected that their quiet "Blooming Boy" was really a girl.

Deborah knew that her mother would worry about her if she did not hear from her. So she wrote a letter saying that she was fine. "I have found work in a large family," she wrote.

"Leave Me, I Am Going to Die!"

That winter, food was hard to get. The soldiers were always hungry. One day Deborah and a few soldiers rode their horses on a scouting party to a cave. The cave was filled with food that had been stolen by the Tories. The Tories planned to give it to the British soldiers.

There were jars of honey in the cave and butter, bacon, and cheese. Deborah and the other soldiers were filling their sacks when the Tories discovered them.

Quickly Deborah got up on her horse and galloped away. The enemy was close behind, firing their guns. Suddenly she felt something warm and wet run down her neck. She touched her neck. Her hand came away bloody.

Then she felt a sharp pain in her leg. Deborah said nothing but she knew that she had been shot. She slid off her horse. All of her strength was gone.

She could hardly take a step and she could not stand alone. She looked down

and saw that her boot was bloody. She had been shot in the leg too.

One of the soldiers stopped to help her. Deborah felt she would rather die than have him find out she was a woman.

"Leave me," she begged him. "Save yourself! I am going to die anyway!"

But the soldier took Deborah up on his horse and rode six miles to a hospital.

There, the doctor gave her wine to drink and bound up her head with a bandage. He gave her extra medicine and more bandages for her neck in case she should need them later.

Then he saw how pale she was and that she could hardly walk.

"Do you have any other wounds?" he asked, looking down at her boots.

"No," she said, her heart going like a cannon.

"Sit down, my young lad," said the doctor. "Your boot says you are lying."

Deborah knew she would have to act quickly. If he discovered she had been shot in the leg, he would make her take her clothes off so that he could remove the bullet. Then he would find out her secret.

"My head is throbbing with pain now," said Deborah. "Could I lie down for a while?"

The doctor led her to a small room. As soon as she was alone, she took out her pocket knife. She would use that knife and also the bandages and the medicine the doctor had given her.

She had to take that bullet out of her leg herself.

The first time she tried, she could not do it. She tried again. The pain was more than she could bear. But if she left the bullet for the doctor to remove, he would find out her secret. That thought gave her the courage to try once more.

This time, almost fainting from the

pain, she dug out the bullet, and ban-
daged her throbbing leg.

She rested as long as she could, but it
was not long enough. The strongest soldier with the same wound would have
been sent home and would not have to
fight any longer.

No one knew how badly Deborah had
been hurt. She didn't say a word to
anyone.

Her leg never healed properly.

In a Cold Attic

Two weeks after she had been shot, she was called to take part in a march.

She started on the march. She was still weak and her leg throbbed with every step she took.

Richard Snow was another sick soldier. He was marching next to Deborah when he suddenly stumbled and fell to the ground.

He could not go on.

Deborah thought fast. She told the officer in charge of the march that she

would get Richard Snow to a nearby farmhouse. She said she would catch up with the others as soon as she could.

The officer agreed. This was Tory country. It was dangerous to stop and wait for one soldier to get better.

The nearest house belonged to a farmer named Van Tassel. He was not very friendly, but he led them up to his cold attic. "It's good enough for soldiers," he said.

Deborah's heart beat fast. "He must

be a Tory," she thought, "or a friend of Tories."

He was. Every night he gave noisy parties for his Tory friends.

Deborah's leg was feeling stronger day by day, but Richard Snow was growing weaker and sicker.

Deborah begged Van Tassel for a straw bed for the dying man.

"The floor is good enough for soldiers," he said.

One day Deborah heard footsteps on the stairs. Her heart jumped, but the voice of a girl made her breathe easier. It was Van Tassel's daughter.

She sneaked up food and water for Deborah and Richard.

But for Richard it was too late.

On the tenth day, he died. Van Tassel's daughter helped Deborah bury him.

Then Deborah set out to find the soldiers.

Discovery

General Paterson had heard of the quiet, brave soldier called Robert Shurtliff. On April 1, he chose Deborah to be his personal orderly. It was a high honor to serve him.

"I was given a good horse and fine equipment," she wrote. "I no longer slept on straw on the damp, cold ground, but on a good feather bed."

At last she could take off her dirty clothes and bathe in private.

In June she was sent to Philadelphia on an important mission. But it was not the time to be in the city. A terrible fever was spreading through Philadelphia. Many people got sick. Many died.

Deborah caught the fever too. One day she fainted and was put into a hospital bed. When she came to, she heard two men fighting over which of her clothes each one of them would take.

"Why, they think I'm dead!" Deborah thought in horror.

It took every bit of her strength to speak, to let the nurse know she was alive.

The nurse rushed to tell the doctor that Robert Shurtliff in bunk 5 whom they thought had died was still alive.

By the time Dr. Binney came, Deborah had sunk back into a coma.

The doctor examined her and discovered her secret!

Dr. Binney discovered that Robert Shurtliff, the young soldier, was really a young woman!

But he never made a single sign that he knew.

He introduced Deborah as Robert Shurtliff to his wife and daughters. He told them about the brave soldier who had had many adventures.

Deborah took walks through the city with Dr. Binney's family. Together they strolled through parks and gardens, went to the theater, and sailed on the Delaware River. She was invited to the fine houses of Philadelphia, still known only as a brave Continental soldier.

September was a good time to be in Philadelphia. The peace treaty had finally been signed in Paris. All Philadelphia was celebrating the end of the war. November 3 was the date set for the soldiers to be sent home to their families.

Deborah grew stronger in Philadelphia. Soon she was well enough to travel.

"Is It Really True?"

Dr. Binney gave her a letter to take back to General Paterson.

When Deborah arrived at the camp in early October, she found General Paterson alone.

She handed him Dr. Binney's letter. She was so afraid of what Dr. Binney had written to the General that she ran out of the room before the General could say a word.

An hour later, General Paterson sent for her.

Deborah was shaking like a leaf. He asked her to sit down. His voice was kind.

"Is it really true?" he said to her.

Her eyes filled with tears. For the first time as a soldier, she felt like sobbing and sobbing.

"What will be my fate, sir," she said, "if I say yes?"

"You have nothing to fear, Bobby — er, whoever you are," General Paterson said. "You have only my admiration and respect."

"Then God forbid that I should try and hide what you now know. Yes. It's true. I am Deborah Sampson."

The General shook his head. He could not believe this strange story.

"Can it really be so?"

"Sir, I have no desire to hide the truth any longer," Deborah said.

Then she thought of a plan and her eyes shone with mischief.

"Please sir, if you will get a dress for me — the fanciest gown you can find — you will see what Deborah Sampson can really look like."

The General did as he was asked.

And when Deborah next stood before him, she did not look anything like Robert Shurtliff, the soldier. She was dressed in a pink gown trimmed with lace and ribbons.

The General was amazed.

"Wait right here," the General cried.

"I'll call the captain. He has seen you every day so he should know you!"

When the captain came in, the General said, "We have a visitor whom you may know. This is Deborah Sampson."

"I should be proud to know her," said the captain, "but I don't."

The two men talked for a while. Then General Paterson asked, "Is there any news of my brave orderly — Robert Shurtliff?"

"I fear that he is dead," the captain said.

"The Revolution is full of miracles," General Paterson said. "And this young lady is one of them. Look at her closely and see if you do not see the face of Robert Shurtliff!"

The captain looked puzzled. *This lovely young lady in her pink gown? Robert Shurtliff, the young soldier?*

"You are making fun of me," the captain said.

"Sir," said Deborah. "I am who I am. Deborah Sampson and Robert Shurtliff. One and the same person."

She began to tell him all the names of the men in his company and about the adventures she had taken part in.

"That's enough," the captain said, shaking his head, "I must believe you now."

Deborah then told the two men why she had enlisted as a soldier and how she had kept her secret.

They took her out to the field where the rest of the soldiers were taking part in the daily drill. But not one man knew that the woman in the pink dress was Bobby, their soldier friend.

Deborah Sampson was discharged from the army on October 25, 1783. She had been in the army for about a year and a half. When she left she was given an excellent record of service.

A Farmer's Wife

That spring Deborah met Benjamin Gannet, a farmer. Shortly after they met they were wed. It was almost two years from the day Deborah had signed up for the army.

Deborah Sampson Gannet who had been a soldier was now a farmer's wife.

Deborah's leg still hurt her. She could not do heavy work around the farm.

Benjamin worked the farm hard and

well. They lived in a comfortable house. Roses and fruit trees flowered in the spring. A small stream flowed nearby.

It should have been a peaceful place for Deborah, after her many adventures.

But Deborah still longed for adventure. She still longed to travel — to know what was beyond the next hill.

Many people had heard about the good land in Ohio. They were moving out West — hundreds of them. Deborah wanted to take part in the move out West too.

"Let's go, Ben," she said to her husband.

He wanted to stay where he was. This land meant a great deal to him. He had worked it hard. He knew every rock, every tree on his land.

They did not go out West.

They stayed in Sharon, Massachusetts. They raised a family of three children — two girls and a boy. Then Deborah took in baby Susanna, whose mother had died. She raised Susanna as though she were her very own child.

Deborah was a gentle mother. She had seen enough of war to know that she hated fighting. Deborah's children grew up to be peaceful and kind.

Adventure Again

Deborah was 41 years old and still restless. Sometimes she taught in a school nearby. But that was not enough for her.

By then, her fame was well known. Her amazing story had begun to be told right after she got out of the army. Her adventures had been printed in a New York newspaper. They were told again in newspapers in Massachusetts.

Everyone wanted to know about Deborah's life as Robert Shurtliff, the soldier.

She gave her first talk in Sharon, her home town. It was a big success.

She decided to give talks in other places — cities like Boston, Providence, New York. Ben did not stop her. But he would not go with her. He would stay home with the children and work on the farm.

Deborah Sampson was one of the first women in this country to travel alone and give talks for money. She made all the travel arrangements and took care of every detail by herself.

She put notices in the local papers.

". . . Tickets may be had at the Court House from 5 o'clock till the performance begins. Price 25 cents, children half price. . . ."

She put on her old uniform and spoke about her adventures. She spoke against war. She told how she felt when she could not help the men around her who had been shot.

"I looked upon these scenes," she said,

"as one looks on a drowning man — without being able to extend a hand."

She said she could not understand why men fought. "My young mind wanted to understand why man should rage against his fellow man, to butcher or to be butchered."

She kept a diary:

"May 5th, 1802: When I entered the hall, I must say I was much pleased at the appearance of the audience. It appeared from almost every face that they were full of unbelief — I mean in regard to my being the person that served in the Revolutionary Army."

She kept a record of the money she had to pay out:

"Albany, August 31, 1802:
To old key keeper 2 00
To Mr. Barber for printing 3 00
To Mr. Lester for finding candles 1 34
To sweeping the court house 0 48

For cleaning the candle sticks	0 20
For brushing the seats	0 17
For the dressing of my hair	1 00
To boarding	6 00
To washing	1 34

Some of the money she earned she sent home. "I hope my family makes good use of it," she wrote.

Sometimes she made visits to her old army friends. Once she stayed at the home of old General Paterson and his wife.

But she began to miss her family more and more.

"O dear, could I but once more see my dear children," she wrote in her diary.

She was getting tired of traveling from one place to the next.

Besides, her leg still hurt her, especially when she was tired.

The next year she came home for good.

Two years later, in 1805, the government voted to give money to the soldiers who had been wounded in the war. Deborah received her share.

Thirteen years later, the government gave her more money. She got $8 a month until she died on April 29, 1827 at the age of 67.

More than a hundred years after she died, she was not forgotten. A warship was named after her.

Today, in Sharon, Massachusetts, the house she lived in with Ben and her children still stands. In the quiet cemetery, a marble tablet has been put up in her honor. Nearby is Deborah Sampson Street, named for the daring young woman who looked for adventure — and found it.

PRAISE FOR

The End of the Alphabet

"*The End of the Alphabet* is a lovely little novel that packs a big emotional wallop. As soon as I finished I called my wife to invite her to an impromptu lunch. It's that kind of book."

—*USA Today*

"*The End of the Alphabet* [is] a sad, sweet debut novella . . . a tear-stained goodbye note and a heartfelt love letter."

—*Los Angeles Times*

"This slim debut novel distills the essence of life and love . . . A novel that can be read in a single sitting of less than two hours might continue to resonate with readers for weeks, months, years to come."

—*Kirkus Reviews*

"[Richardson] writes with such visual and emotional density that the end of the reading readily becomes the start of another."

—*Globe and Mail*

"Nothing less than gorgeous, a short and intense novel structured around the beautiful cul de sac of the alphabet itself . . . The story is irresistible . . . Evocative and unforgettable, it manages to arouse both a longing for travel and a longing for home."

—*Calgary Herald*

THE END

OF

THE ALPHABET

CS RICHARDSON

BROADWAY BOOKS

New York

For Rebecca . . . T . M . D .

Copyright © 2007 by Dravot & Carnehan, Inc.

All Rights Reserved

Published in the United States by Broadway Books,
an imprint of The Doubleday Publishing Group,
a division of Random House, Inc., New York.
www.broadwaybooks.com

The End of the Alphabet was originally published in Canada
by Doubleday, Toronto, in 2007. A hardcover edition of this book
was published in the United States in 2007 by Doubleday.

BROADWAY BOOKS and its logo, a letter B bisected on the diagonal,
are trademarks of Random House, Inc.

Book design by Judith Stagnitto Abbate/Abbate Design

Library of Congress Cataloging-in-Publication Data
Richardson, CS
The end of the alphabet / CS Richardson.
p. cm.
I. Self-realization—Fiction. 2. Voyages around the world—Fiction.
I. Title.
PR9199.4.R5237E53 2007
823'.92—dc22   2006036823

ISBN 978-0-7679-2763-5

PRINTED IN THE UNITED STATES OF AMERICA

1 3 5 7 9 10 8 6 4 2

First Paperback Edition

Think of the long trip home.
Should we have stayed at home
and thought of here?
Where should we be today?

ELIZABETH BISHOP,
"Questions of Travel"

This story is unlikely.

Were it otherwise, or at the least more wished for, it would have begun on a Sunday morning. Early, as that was his best time of the day, and in April, that odd time between a thin winter and a plump spring.

He would have closed the door of his house and stood on his front step, eyeing the predawn sky. He would have given the neighborhood stray a shove from its perch on his window ledge. The scruffy cat would have hissed and bolted across the narrow road to the park across the way. He would have hissed back, proud he had at last defeated the mangy beast, and set off. As he had every Sunday morning as far back as he could remember.

As he walked up the road, the woman from number eighteen would be retrieving the morning paper from her doorstep. The cool morning would have meant she had remembered to throw on a dressing gown. They would have traded pleasant, awkward good mornings. He knew her to be the mother of two energetic children whose names he could never recall. She knew he worked in some sort of creative field. After a moment or two of searching for common ground, he would have asked after her children's artwork. He and his wife had no children of their own.

Farther on, he would have seen the elderly man and his tiny dog, who lived at number twelve, about to begin their morning walk around the park. The pair would be waiting to say hello. The man would have tipped his cap and launched directly into an eccentric opinion about something. The tiny dog would have begun yapping at the neighborhood stray.

He would have worried about disagreeing with the old fellow and causing offense or starting a discussion on a topic he knew nothing about or the soundness of his own opinion. He would have forced an agreeing laugh, wished his neighbor a good day, and eyed the dog with suspicion.

He would have made his way to Kensington High Street and grumbled about the winter that had passed. He would have wished he had taken his wife to Italy. But that would have been expensive or difficult or meant a bad time at the office. He would have sighed to himself, then smiled as the London sky inched from black to gray to yellow to blue.

He would have turned in at Kensington Gardens, up past the palace and on to Broad Walk. Here he would have been happiest. He would have paused near the Round Pond, looked toward the east and the swans, and squinted in his way to watch a girl of perhaps nine or ten, her hair dark and fine and in need of a trim or a ribbon, reading a book beyond her years. He would have closed his eyes in the warmth of a sun just clearing the budding treetops.

He would have checked his watch, counted his minutes and the day's schedule in his head, and turned for home. He would have retraced his route down the Walk, past the palace, along the High Street, into his road, past number twelve and number eighteen and the cat now back on the window ledge, and through his front door.

His wife would have begun to stir in her sleep. Five minutes more, she would have mumbled, just loud enough for him to hear as he made her tea. As usual, a tepid cup with too much milk.

Ambrose Zephyr would have been content

that it was Sunday and that spring had come again to that part of London and that there was no need to go to the office. He would have read a draft of his wife's latest magazine column and (as gentle readers are obliged) made one or two enthusiastic comments.

He would have wondered about the days ahead of him and, as was his habit, dreamed of doing something else. And there it would have ended.

But that is not this story.

On or about his fiftieth birthday, Ambrose
Zephyr failed his annual medical exam. An
illness of inexplicable origin with neither known
nor foreseeable cure was discovered. It would
kill him within the month. Give or take a day.

It was suggested he might want to make
arrangements concerning his remaining time.

Ambrose Zephyr lived with his wife—content, quiet, with few extravagances—in a narrow Victorian terrace full of books.

He owned two bespoke suits, one of which he had been married in. The other—a three-piece linen number with lapelled waistcoat—he wore whenever and wherever he traveled: on business, on the underground, on his Sunday walk. A pocket square, discreetly puffed, always in place. He collected French-cuffed shirts as others might collect souvenir spoons or back issues of *National Geographic*. He rarely wore ties but liked them as challenges in graphic design. His footwear was predominantly Italian, loaferish, and bought in the sales on Oxford Street. His watches—of which there were many—were a range of silly colors and eccentric shapes.

———

When cornered, he claimed to read Joyce, Ford, and Conrad. Rereads of Fleming and Wodehouse were a more accurate library. His opinion of Miss Elizabeth Bennet was not favorable (though he liked Mr. B. and held a wary respect for Darcy). *Wuthering Heights,* according to Ambrose, was the dullest book ever written.

He had not read a newspaper in some time.

Everything Ambrose Zephyr knew about cuisine he learned from his wife. He was allowed in the kitchen, but under no circumstances was he to touch anything. He was a courageous eater, save Brussels sprouts and clams. His knowledge of wine was vague and best defined as Napa good, Australian better, French better still. Kir royale was his drink of occasion. For an Englishman, he made a poor cup of tea.

He believed women to be quantifiably wiser than men. He was neither a breast nor a leg nor an ass man; hair could be any length, any color. Ambrose preferred the complete puzzle to a bit here, a piece there.

He stood when someone entered the room. He walked at the street side. Opened his wife's door first. He could be trusted.

———

Ambrose Zephyr worked as the creative wallah
for Dravot, Carnehan. Ill-mannered
competitors termed it the D&C. Messrs. Dravot
and Carnehan had long ago divested their
interests in the advertising agency to a
globalizing media concern. The principals then
went off to seek other fortunes and left Ambrose
working for a wise and exhausted woman
named Greta.

Coworkers considered Ambrose to possess
an inventive if journeyman approach to the
creative process: on time, on budget, realistic,
reasonable. He was neither star nor guru.
Ambrose was comfortable with that. A client is
in the business of selling something, he often
said, but that something is usually not Ambrose
Zephyr.

With his heels to the wall Ambrose stood an inch
or two under six feet. Excluding the inevitable
middle-years droop of waist and waddle, his
frame was thinnish. His head, well seasoned,
carried the same amount of hair it did when he
was a boy. His eyes were creased at the corners
and as blue as the day when, fifty years before, a
young and sad Queen had come home from
Africa.

Those who knew him described Ambrose Zephyr as a better man than some. Wanting a few minor adjustments, they would admit, but didn't we all. His wife described him as the only man she had loved. Without adjustment.

Indeed, said the doctor. Arrangements.

Ambrose Zephyr suggested, for all in the
outer office to hear, that the doctor might want
to wait one damn minute before suggesting that
Ambrose might want to arrange his remaining
days. Days that until moments before had been
assumed would stretch to years. With luck, to
decades. Not shrink to weeks.

If that, said the doctor.

The room filled with fog. The doctor became
a blurry lump behind the desk. The air turned
as thick as custard, sauna hot. Ambrose
struggled to keep his questions from spilling
out with his breakfast in a puddle on the floor.

Something of a mystery, answered the
doctor.

Not contagious as far as we can tell.

Fatal? Yes, quite.

Very sure.

≡

Ambrose Zephyr was married to Zappora
Ashkenazi, a woman as comfortable in her own
skin as anyone else. She had kept her name for
the apparent reasons, would have preferred to
have been born a Frenchwoman, suffered fools
with grace and a smile, loathed insects.

She had decorated the Victorian terrace in
tastefully Swedish DIY, updating as budget and
wear dictated. She was resigned to the likelihood
that a pied-à-terre in the sixth arrondissement
might not be in her future. She was content with
that.

She wore the best labels she could afford and
knew the mysteries that moved a £500 ensemble
to the £50 rack. Red and black and white were
her colors. Accessorizing she considered well
worth the effort, and her earrings were almost
always perfect with that outfit. She owned one
pair of stilettoed shoes that hurt just to look at.
But Ambrose liked them. Which was enough.

She read everything. Russian epics, French confections, American noir, English tabloids had at one time or another taken their place in a wobbly pile beside the bed. Nonfiction was too much like school, she said. Experimental literature left her cold and annoyed and despairing for the so-called modern craft. She had lost count of how many times she had read *Wuthering Heights*.

She could walk into a kitchen she had never seen before and—without a recipe—plate a meal worthy of a starred review in half the time it took her husband to find an egg to boil. Her kitchen was full of cookery books that had never felt the splash of an errant sauce. She read them, she displayed them; they felt good in hand. They completed the room. Like earrings.

Men brought out her best and made her laugh. She liked most beards, hated all mustaches, and furrowed her brow at the mention of tattoos. Height and weight and size didn't matter. Manners and nice shoes mattered. Doing the better thing mattered.

Her shoulder was ready when friends felt a cry coming on. She knew where to offer opinion and when to shut up. She could juggle oranges. She lied only a little, and they were always white.

Zappora Ashkenazi was the literary editor for the country's third-most-read fashion magazine. Her publisher had wanted to introduce the magazine's reluctant readership to both new and classic literature, and if that literature held a passing link to couture, so much the better. It was a job with challenge: Austen, Woolf, and Parker had never, so far as Zappora knew, assembled a spring collection. Yet those who read "On the Nightstand" every month did so faithfully and first. Her writing was known for its economic style and refreshing avoidance of simile. Her husband was her first reader. Every word, every draft. You always have an interesting story to tell, he would say.

Zappora started in the fashion trade as a photographer's dresser. She flipped collars, fanned skirts, hitched pants, buttoned, tied, zipped. By the end of the first hour with her first model on her first day of her first real job she was given her first nickname.

Zipper.

She was very proud.

Zipper was not quite as tall as her husband, not quite as thin, and not quite as old. Her hair was dark and fine and trimmed precisely every eight weeks. Colored, perhaps tied with a ribbon, as required.

Her eyes were creased at the corners. She wore glasses when reading. The glasses were purchased in a small shop in Paris, around the corner from an antiquarian bookshop.

Zipper sat silent beside her husband, thinking how curious it was that her body had stopped working. That the doctor sounded like he was speaking underwater.

She wondered what would happen if she got up and left. Better yet, hadn't come in at all. She clung to the sense of it.

I am not in the room.

Ambrose is not unraveling into the sweating, pasty stranger sitting next to me.

We are at home, preparing a meal for friends or deciding which film to see or selecting which book to curl up with or standing on the doorstep watching that annoying cat with those stupid birds.

We are not here.

None of this is happening to us.

Depending on the storyteller, Ambrose and Zipper met for the first or second time in the offices of Dravot, Carnehan. The third-most-read fashion magazine in the country was at the time a fledgling and unread concept. It was being pitched to the city's advertising community in an effort to change that.

Messrs. Dravot and Carnehan sat at one end of their unnecessarily long boardroom table. Ambrose stood in a corner trying to look creative. He was the only man in the room not wearing a tie. The magazine's presentation team was led by a painfully loud publisher and trailed by a nervous junior editor, introduced as Young Ms. Ashkenazi Who I Believe Will Be Heading Up Our Literary Efforts.

Ambrose would later admit to a nagging sensation of having seen this Ms. Ashkenazi before. How he could not place her, but that her handshake felt small, warm, a touch damp. How he could not take his eyes off her. And how, more than once, he had narrowed his gaze to watch her, topless, eating tapas on a beach in Spain. She might have been twenty, maybe twenty-one years old. It was hard to see clearly, Ambrose would explain, what with the sun and the heat and the glare off the sea.

Zipper had an equally odd feeling throughout the meeting. She thought, but couldn't be sure, that she knew the slightly handsome man in the corner who said nothing. (What she never mentioned to anyone was the pleasant hum she felt as Ambrose spent the meeting trying not to glance at her breasts. Or that she found his periodic squint boyishly charming.)

Looking back, Ambrose and Zipper agreed the meeting could not have ended soon enough. As we'll-be-in-touch's went around the room, Ambrose complimented Ms. Ashkenazi on her glasses. In that moment Zipper recalled where she had seen this man before.

Coffee? Ambrose then suggested.

It's Zappora. Zipper, actually.

But if you'd rather not . . .

Zipper smiled.

You're busy then . . . not to worry. Right. *Zipper?* Well. Yes. Lovely. Perhaps another time . . . Have we met? No, my mistake. There you are. Sorry. Right. Well.

Zipper remembered the rain in Paris. Tea would be brilliant, she said.

Ambrose escorted the magazine team to the street. While everyone waited for taxis and compared notes for their next presentation, Zipper conjured a case of performance nerves and told the team she'd catch up. Ambrose never went back to the office.

They spent the rest of the morning and the better part of the afternoon in a tiny café near Seven Dials. The next day a grinning Ambrose turned up at D&C at noon, wearing a shambled version of the clothes he had worn the day before.

Ambrose Zephyr later claimed that Zipper was the only woman he had ever been honest with. Not that he had ever misled anyone (perhaps a mild fib here and there), but with Zipper there would be no showing off, no blurring of unfortunate detail, no exaggeration for effect. In the face of all reason, she was interested in him as he was. Not as he wished he was.

From that morning across the boardroom table, or earlier—depending on the storyteller— on a narrow street in Paris, Ambrose and Zipper were almost effortless.

They were married beside an anonymous willow near the statue of Peter Pan.

It was a small, drenched affair. All parents attended, as uncomfortable as newly met in-laws can be but managing to find common ground in grumbles about the weather, the venue, the damned informality of it all. A blown lightbulb from the recently acquired and completely bare Victorian terrace was broken under foot.

The following week a notice ran in the social pages of the Sunday editions:

> ZEPHYR/ASHKENAZI. Saturday last, at Kensington Gardens. Ambrose Zephyr (Esq.) and Zappora Ashkenazi (Ms.), attended by Katerina Mankowitz (Ms.) of Bayswater and Frederick Wilkes (Esq.) of Her Majesty's Foreign Office. The bride, who will retain her maiden name, wore a vintage ensemble in off-white, tailored by Umtata's of Old Jewry. The couple is currently honeymooning on the continent. Their long-term plans were not available at press time.

Why you? Why anyone? responded the doctor.

I'm afraid not. Nothing to be done.

Unlikely, but perhaps.

Could be, but doubtful.

How long? Thirty days. Give or take.

Faculties may dull a bit. Blurred eyesight, ringing ears, numbed fingertips. That sort of thing. Happens rather quickly as far as we can tell.

Yes, the doctor offered, unfair would be a very good word about now.

Ambrose Zephyr's father toiled as a wordsmith for one of the more popular broadsheets of the day. Not long after writing his son's wedding notice, he had taken an early retirement. Enough reading about it, he told his wife.

Mr. Zephyr died five days later. His heart had stopped as he walked to the corner shop for milk and the day's papers. There was no good reason, said the coroner.

Ambrose's mother called her son at the offices of D&C. When Ambrose rang off, he threw his collection of antique type blocks across the room. They shattered the window separating him from the creative department. He sat there, surrounded by bits of glass and stared at by the younger talents in the office, for most of the morning.

In the months that followed, Mrs. Zephyr took to calling her son at all hours, moaning about this ache or that pain. She began complaining about her tea, convinced someone had changed the mixture after two hundred years and how dare the bastards. She whined about the Queen.

On the good days Ambrose would offer, as pleasantly as he could, to take his mother to the National Gallery. Too crowded, she said. What's on the telly? Not *that* tea.

One Sunday afternoon, Ambrose stopped by for a visit. He found his mother sitting on the floor in her kitchen, surrounded by a week's worth of newspapers, whimpering at the mess around her.

I can't remember his face, she said.

A neighbor called Ambrose the next day to say his mother had passed quietly in her sleep. That evening, for the first time since he was old enough to read, Ambrose Zephyr did not look at a newspaper. There were other things happening in the world.

Ambrose Zephyr sat dumb and frozen on his front step. He may have seen something like the elderly man from number twelve carrying his tiny dog around the park. Or number eighteen returning from work, her children bouncing on the pavement and brandishing their day's art. Or the neighborhood stray rousing from its spot on the window ledge and strolling defiantly toward the birds.

Ambrose and Zipper made something like love that night. It was rough, frantic, tearful, quick. Ambrose rolled away and went downstairs without saying a word. Zipper lay perfectly still, staring at the ceiling. Tears trickled into her ears. She thought she could hear her husband shaking in the dark.

Ambrose Zephyr began life a loved if overshadowed baby. Mrs. Zephyr's labor started while she was listening to the radio: the King was dead and his daughter, now a young and sad queen, was returning from Kenya. Mr. Zephyr was delayed at the office—a new queen did not come along every day—and could not meet his son until the special edition had started coming off the presses.

Not so many years later, on a Saturday evening, Mr. Zephyr took young Ambrose to the newspaper's offices. He showed his son the collection of retired wood and lead typefaces on display in the lobby. Young Ambrose liked the way the small type blocks felt large and heavy in his hand. He liked the tidy way each type was organized—one letter, one cubby—in a large flat wooden drawer. At the same time, he was angry that Z lived in such a small space compared to A. It isn't fair, he said with a dark scowl.

His father tut-tutted. Such is the manner of alphabets, he said. Some types are luckier than others. A may have more space in the drawer, but Z is no less important, particularly when it comes to words like zebra.

Or Zephyr, said Ambrose, straightening his small back.

Or Zanzibar, said his father. A place very far away.

A place with *two* z's?

Indeed. And two a's.

I think I would like that place, said Ambrose.

Mrs. Zephyr worked as a junior art appraiser for a large and prestigious auction house. The art she usually appraised was neither. When her son was eight or perhaps nine she took him on his first visit to the National Gallery. To see the proper stuff, she said.

She explained all that they saw: who the artist was, where the painting had come from, how old or new it was, who the people on the canvases were. Ambrose found some of the paintings boring, particularly those with snobby children in satin suits and silly collars. He liked the paintings that featured a lot of blood. Or people dying. This preference he kept from his mother.

Ambrose also noticed quite a few paintings of naked women. Lying on beds, wrestling with naked men, holding haloed babies, admiring themselves in mirrors. Ambrose wondered whether artists ever got erections as they painted these women. This question he also kept from his mother.

When Mrs. Zephyr started talking about the school of this or the ism of that, Ambrose stopped listening. To him what he saw was what it was. Some paintings made him wonder, some made him giggle, some made him squirm. The Dutch Master with his floppy clown hat and thin beard and bright eyes, the chubby girls with their chubby dogs, the giant sunflowers drooping out of their pot like alien plant people with one bulging green eye.

. . . painted by a troubled young man, Mrs. Zephyr was saying, . . . cut off part of his own ear . . .

Ambrose went back to looking. What he saw didn't need his mother going on about symbols and meanings and madness and genius, he thought. She knew a lot, but she didn't know when to stop complicating things.

The sunflowers were like none he had ever seen, ear or no ear, troubles or not.

Ambrose Zephyr liked what he liked and didn't like what he didn't like.

It was as simple as that.

———

Zipper woke to what felt like something heavy being dragged from under her, mingled with the sound of her husband's whispers.

Must go now . . . leave today . . . no time . . . no waiting . . . arrangements . . . places to be . . . a list . . . A is for . . .

Ambrose was naked. Sweat dripped off him as he rummaged under the bed. The large suitcase snagged on the bedsprings. He pulled it free and in the same motion threw it on the bed.

Austria? . . . no . . . B for Belize? . . . no . . . people to see . . . things must be done . . . make a list . . . have a plan . . . go now . . . C is for . . .

It was a square and handsome case: oxblood leather, reinforced corners, brass hinges. A thick handle. A man's handle. It looked like it had never been used for anything other than storage.

As a boy, Ambrose Zephyr was considered by the neighbors to be well mannered, agreeable, and quiet. Average was a word often used. That is, they said, aside from the travel brochures. And the alphabets.

He spent days alone in his room, compiling addresses for every embassy, mission, and consulate in London. He wrote letters, in his best hand, to each ambassador or commissioner or consul explaining that he was planning to visit their country in the very near future and would Sir or Madam be so kind as to possibly forward any and all information concerning their fine country at the earliest possible convenience yours very sincerely Master Ambrose Zephyr Esq. He worked for hours perfecting the proper amount of swoosh to his Z's.

On one wall of his room he had taped a large map (which the Prime Minister's office had forwarded after Ambrose had inquired about the nations of the Commonwealth and was there, Mr. Prime Minister, Sir, a particular reason why each was shaded pink?). Ambrose stuck redheaded pins in the places that replied with the glossiest literature. Within a few weeks, Switzerland became a small red hedgehog popping from the top of an Italian boot.

When he wasn't corresponding with dignitaries, Ambrose Zephyr was drawing. A's through Z's. In the hundreds. Twenty-six at a time, plus punctuation, numerals, and ampersands.

Some of his alphabets were illustrated with less popular members of the animal world: *A is for anaconda, B is for booby, C is for codfish*. Some depicted the world on his map: *D is for a beach in the Dutch Antilles, E is for the windy coast of Elba, F is for palm trees in Florida*. Some combined the two themes: *G is for geckos in the German woods, H is for Hellenic capybaras in a taverna, I is for Italian bats in the Vatican belfry*. When his father asked why A wasn't apple or B wasn't bird or C wasn't cat, young Ambrose explained that things didn't always have to be the way you'd expect.

Everybody does apples and birds and cats, he said, and it's boring to do what everybody else does and I'm not much good at drawing cats anyway, I can never get the feet right.

A list of what? said Zipper.

   . . . Calcutta . . . sorry? whispered Ambrose. List? Yes. What?

   Come back to bed.

   Places . . . things . . .

   What things?

   Places . . . A is for . . .

   Zipper pulled the duvet and her knees to her chin and watched her husband empty the suitcase. Scores of brochures, advertisements, maps, booklets, supplements, catalogs, and flyers spilled onto the bed. Together with hundreds of drawings: some childish and faded, others by a more accomplished hand. All of them letters. A through Z. Everything formed a small mountain on the bed and spilled onto the floor.

   Where? said Zipper.

   Things, said Ambrose.

   Like?

Places. A to Z equals twenty-six. A month
equals thirty. The doctor said as much. Or is it
twenty-nine? What year is this? Twenty-eight?
A month, give or take.

I know what the doctor said. Are you all
right?

Fine.

Then come back to bed.

What would you do?

What?

DO. What. Would. You. Do.

About what?

Time, time, time. Thirty days. No time.
Weren't you listening?

Don't ask me that.

Tea came and went as Zipper reviewed her
husband's list. *Places . . . Things. 1) A is for a
portrait in Amsterdam. . . .* There was no mention
of putting affairs in order, no alternative
remedies, no sprinkling of ashes under an
anonymous willow in Kensington Gardens.
Zipper's mind spun. This was not her Ambrose,
she thought at first. But then, apparently, it was.

Paris being so far down the list and what
happened after Zanzibar and why was X blank
and how and what with and what if and are you

mad and should we and shouldn't we and how could you and don't do this don't *be* this don't go without me don't go at all were thoughts Zipper fought to keep down.

Instead, she frowned and suggested that Andalusia might be nicer this time of year.

Habitually (in blind panic, she would later admit), Zipper edited. She penciled a stroke through Valparaíso, a place she had never heard of, and in the margin wrote *Venice*.

The love they made that morning was tender, lingering, and generous. She before he.

After, they talked of the Bridge of Sighs.

A

The ferry from Harwich crossed a rough and cold
sea. The passage did not agree with Zipper, and she
spent most of it belowdecks. Ambrose, waved off
for useless hovering, spent most of it at the railing,
watching the lights along the European shore grow
brighter on the horizon. They ate lunch the next day
in a café at the edge of a pretty square in Amsterdam.

Ambrose was dressed in his linen travel
number: hastily pressed, pocket squared. Zipper
in a white cotton blouse and black trousers cut
in a capri style. Ambrose had always admired the
way her back moved in that outfit. Her shoes
were comfortable. Red.

Amid sips of coffee and suggested itineraries,
Zipper remembered a conversation.

Lovely, she said.
Sorry. What? Ambrose said.

The Velázquez.

Sorry? Yes.

They had been married most of a year. Having coaxed Ambrose into taking her on one of his usually solitary visits to the National Gallery, Zipper had done some reading beforehand.

Venus at Her Mirror, Zipper said.

The Rokeby Venus, said Ambrose.

The model was somebody's mistress?

The King of Spain. Philip, I think.

Had a thing for black taffeta sheets.

The King?

The mistress. And didn't a suffragette attack her with a knife?

The mistress?

The painting. Are you listening?

Right. Yes.

It's the sheets, Zipper said. They highlight the form. Her form. And Velázquez painted her hazy reflection in the mirror on purpose. Forces the eye to the form. Sorry, her form. Critics said the reflection looked unfinished. The optics were wrong. We should be seeing her torso reflected in the mirror. How am I doing?

Sorry. Yes. Lovely.

What, precisely, is so lovely?

Her. This. The Velázquez.

Why?

Because it is.

That's it?

I think so. Yes.

You're impossible, Zipper said. All I know is what I've read. All I'd like to know is what you know. What you think.

About what?

About why, damn it. Why the sheets and the optics and the mistress and the unfinished reflection? Why love it so much? Why her?

It is what it is, said Ambrose. Lovely.

You're exhausting.

Fine. If you insist, it reminds me of you.

Really. My backside is not nearly so lovely.

I wasn't looking at her backside.

Really.

I was looking at her front. The slope of the neck. Curve of the breasts, the smooth stomach. The gentle hollow around the navel. Her face.

You're imagining things.

Isn't that the point?

They thought better of visiting the Rijksmuseum together.

Zipper said she wasn't sure how she would

spend the day. Ambrose did his best to reassure.
There was, he said, no need to worry. They
kissed and Ambrose set off to find a portrait
he had seen before. But long ago and from very
far away.

A younger Ambrose arrived behind his time,
having spent most of the previous day in the pub
with Freddie Wilkes.

It was the oldest lecture theater on campus:
a cavernous circular space with graceful
plasterwork, smelling of mold and varnish and
nervous sweat. The few windows it had were
small, painted forever shut, and set high behind
tiers of hard benches worn by a century or two
of first-term buttocks.

Ambrose found a seat in the back rows and
consulted his schedule. "The Place of the
Portrait." Below him the professor paced the
dais, a small man gesturing with a long pointer
at his latest slide: a Rembrandt, late in the
artist's career. The reproduction was poor. The
slide was scratched from years of projection, the
contrast blown, the detail flattened to blobs.

It was a group portrait. *The Company of Captain
Frans Banning Cocq and Lieutenant Willem van Ruytenburch*,
announced the professor. Painted in 1642. You
may, if you must, call it *The Night Watch*.

Captain Cocq's company—by the professor's pointed count—consisted of thirty-five adults, two children, one chicken, and one dog, as well as various lances, spears, pikes, walking canes, drums, flags, and muskets.

The professor rambled at length about dynamic magnetism and profound insight and asymmetric composition. NOTE, IF YOU WILL, he kept yelling . . . the significance of this . . . symbolism of that . . . transcendence of genre . . . portrait of genius . . .

Ambrose raised his thick head and stared at the projection. Not once had the professor mentioned a shadowed half face, hardly visible behind the painted crowd, peeking back at Ambrose with a pair of bright and smiling eyes.

In a grand and old department store Zipper wandered from floor to floor. Here a blouse held to her chest and rehung on its rack; there the silk of a scarf, fingered and left folded. She sampled a lipstick that matched, precisely, the color of her shoes. Assistants asked if madam required help. Zipper felt her eyes water and managed no thank you. She left the store without buying anything.

She came across a small bookshop in a tilted narrow building. A sign in the window

advertised Gently Read Literature, Items for
Composition and Correspondence Within.
Zipper shuffled around the shop, finally settling
on a small leather journal, rounded at the
corners. An envelope for keeping reminders
and receipts and bits of things was bound inside
the back cover, a thick elastic band held all in
place. The proprietor was still counting change
as Zipper ran out of the shop.

She struggled to catch her breath, needed to
sit down, went cold, thought she was going to
vomit. She found a bench overlooking a canal
and sat on her hands to hide the tremors. She
stared at a passing tourist barge, her eyes filling
with panic as those on board practiced ducking
under footbridges yet to come.

The shaking stopped as suddenly as it had
begun. Zipper had nothing to wipe her eyes.
Flustered, she used the sleeve of her blouse. She
stood, unsure of her knees, and headed off to
meet her husband at the train station.

Ambrose Zephyr reviewed the departures board,
confirmed the overnight train would be leaving
on time, and made his way to the platform to
meet his wife. If someone were no wiser, he
might have looked as content as a man on
holiday.

Zipper watched her husband approach. Relieved at his relaxed way, she closed her journal. A souvenir postcard—a garish reproduction of a group portrait by Rembrandt—peeked from the envelope inside the cover. Ambrose paid no attention. He was too busy telling his story.

. . . bigger than I expected. Enormous. More like a company of giants . . . There he was, behind the watchmen, the children, the chicken, the dog, the lances and spears and pikes and canes, the drums, the flags, the muskets . . . the master himself, peeking over a shoulder with those laughing eyes, I swear they winked . . .

Ambrose flailed and paced like an awkward conductor.

. . . and sweep and swirl and banners and action and such a good Rembrandt and luscious and bold and warm and thick with amazing outfits . . . the lieutenant in yellow of all things . . .

Ambrose caught his breath.

. . . and the genius?

Zipper ventured a guess. His use of light?

Work for hire, said Ambrose. Commissioned and paid for by the captain et al. Hah! *There's* your genius. There's the art.

Zipper smiled. Until then, she had always assumed the Rembrandt was what it was.

On the night train to Berlin, Ambrose slept as well as anyone sitting upright on a train might. Zipper sat clutching the journal until her hands went clammy. She tried opening it a few times. A thousand words flew through her head but she couldn't manage to land any on the page.

After a while she gave up and watched the dark-gray countryside speed past her reflection in the window.

B

They sat at an outdoor table on the Unter den
Linden. The sky was clear, blue, welcoming.
The lime trees showed an early-spring green and
offered comfortable shade.

Nearby stood a brooding Brandenburg Gate,
all heavy stone and column. Tourists and locals
and friends and lovers were enjoying the
morning, strolling through the gate as if it
weren't there.

Zipper Ashkenazi's legs stretched from under
her, her shoes off. She watched a street
entertainer prepare for the day's performance:
unfolding a music stand, tuning a battered
violin. She had passed a poor night, but on this
morning and in this place she was content.

Ambrose stewed. He knew he needed to be
here. He knew he needed to get past this. He
knew it would make Zipper happy. But still he
fussed and squirmed in search of a comfortable

place in his chair. He kept an eye on the gate and scowled.

He claimed he was only thinking of his uncle, but Zipper knew there was more to it than that.

At one time or another, Ambrose had spoken of his Uncle Jack. How he had taught an annoyingly inquisitive nephew the subtleties of life. The first gentleman I ever met, Ambrose would say.

Every Remembrance Sunday, Jack came up to the city, wearing the same threadbare jacket and regimental tie he had worn the year before. His shoes always shone, he smelled freshly shaved, he stood whenever Mrs. Zephyr entered or left the room. He had an unsure smile that matched his limp.

One particular November, young Ambrose asked his uncle about the war. What had he done? Where had he been?

All over, said Jack. France, Holland, Berlin.

That's right. Germany.

Wasn't very nice.

People weren't very nice either.

Didn't like us, I suppose. They didn't like a lot of people.

They did. People they'd no business killing.

Friends? A few.

No. I didn't help my friends. I was away.

A few years later at his uncle's funeral, Ambrose read about someone named Sylvia. She had died when an air raid blew up her house near Spitalfields. Jack had left her a note, apologizing for not being there. For not keeping her safe.

Zipper knew that, with odd exception, Ambrose held a modern view of the world. He kept himself informed well enough, knew there was neither black nor white, believed what the BBC told him. Yet when she reminisced about her younger location-shoot days in Germany, she could watch his view become as black and blind as ash. With an unnerving Berlin at its center.

In its grayness. The weather always threatening, the streets always wet. The architecture all cold stone: large and hard and lacking in windows.

With its inhabitants. Sour and stiff with permanently furrowed expressions. They spoke a jarring language: phlegmy, incapable of expressions of love. No one smiled. Laughter was faked. There never seemed to be any children.

With its music. Unlistenable. Funereal. Loud.

And its ghosts. Prowling, wearing uniforms, black, brown, gray. Lurking in doorways, dropping bombs on houses, burning Zipper's books. Watching and waiting to steal her away.

That was then, Zipper said. Jack was then.

She pulled Ambrose to his feet, and they set off to walk the city she knew.

They made their way through the Reichstag. Once an asylum run by madmen, now through its center an atrium of glass and mirror poured sky into the building and warmed Ambrose's upturned face.

They visited the zoo, where people had once eaten the animals left behind. On this day it was full of children, laughing at the monkeys, waving at the pandas, having their photographs taken by tired parents.

Along more than one boulevard Ambrose and Zipper jostled past crowded coffee bars and neon dance clubs and persistent Gypsy beggars; bored fashion models and charged young lovers and old people with old dogs; graffiti artists and boisterous hawkers and women for sale and men who smiled like cartoon spies and made Ambrose chuckle.

They walked, perhaps a little lost, along Oranienburgerstrasse and through an ancient neighborhood. They asked directions from a young man with a long and unkempt beard. He mumbled through his whiskers and pointed vaguely down the street. Zipper thanked him in the only Yiddish she could recall. The man grinned and shuffled Ambrose and Zipper along their way.

As dusk came, they returned to the avenue under the lime trees. The street performer was calling for last requests. Ambrose watched a woman in tailored red trousers and a black turtleneck approach the violinist. She whispered in his ear. The performer bowed and played the opening notes of the woman's request. She turned to her companion, a reluctant gentleman with graying hair, and offered her hand. The couple danced to a waltz composed by a German whose name Ambrose could not recall.

This is now, Zipper said, as she picked up a small stone and slid it in her pocket. The sky grew dark and the stars came out.

Ambrose smiled and asked if she had said something. If she was safe. If she was happy.

C

As the high-speed train crossed into France, its vending machines served Ambrose Zephyr a breakfast of stale croissant and muddy coffee. He checked his watch, took a measure of the fields whizzing past the window, and announced to his wife that an improved lunch would, with luck, be served in Chartres.

Zipper declined breakfast for the apparent reasons. In silence she fretted over maths: days spent, days remaining, days to come. Couldn't we just stay in one place, she thought. *C rhymes with P.* Which stood for Paris. Too many letters and too many days away.

She tried thinking of clever ways to rearrange the alphabet. Her brain refused the work. Instead, she imagined a proper meal and a change of clothes, a nap in a quiet spot near the river, a view of the cathedral. At the least, food or fresh underwear or rest would pass the time while Ambrose attended church.

———

He was fond of repeatedly telling the story of his best day in advertising. A day, so the story began, when Ambrose Zephyr informed a client that they didn't need any advertising.

The client was a little church in the midst of London. For a hundred years or more, it had served its congregation plainly and true. But times—as are their custom—had changed. The parish had retired to the country and filled itself with a more distracted demographic. Those who worshipped at all were doing so in a score of different ways. The little church had fallen on competitive days.

A young priest was newly arrived in the parish and, in the way of the young and the new, saw an opportunity to make his mark. To put the arses, he whispered to Ambrose at their first meeting, back in the pews.

Ambrose was vague on church business. As a boy, he had attended Sunday lessons perhaps once or twice that he could recall. He was cinematically familiar with a few biblical stories. But he knew well the first law of his profession: walk in thy client's shoes. A tour of the little church was decided upon.

It stood, small and quiet and tucked away at

the end of a noisy lane, surrounded by office blocks of glass and steel and looming business. Inside, three pews sat on either side of the aisle. Each pew held a sprig of fresh flowers. Changed every other day, said the priest with much pride. Whatever the market had in bloom. On this day the nave smelled of lavender.

A simple cross was placed on the altar, itself a plain wooden desk. A round window tucked among the rafters above the altar provided as much sunlight as could find its way between the office towers.

Someone had painted a pastel blue sky on the ceiling. Here and there a cloud. Angels, cherubim, beams of light were nowhere to be found. Around the walls were twelve tiny stained glass windows. Those, boasted the priest, were new.

Ambrose expected the windows to hold the usual scenes, rendered in heavy glass with thick colors and serious overtones. Instead, they were as graceful as locket portraits. One depicted a young mother with a pushchair. In another a team of small boys played football. Here was a wedding party. There a lovers' kiss. An old man walking in a park with his dog, a tearful good-bye, a welcome home. The windows were the stations of a life, but the life was anyone's.

Ambrose spent a long time with the young priest's windows, quietly moving around the nave and saying nothing. Finally the priest cleared his throat and broached the subject of professional opinion. Where do we begin? he asked.

A party, answered Ambrose.

A party?

With a bar. Music, all kinds. Food, all kinds. Games for the children. Fun.

A *party*?

Any day but Sunday.

Ambrose's story always ended with the dashing of a young priest's hopes. Television time and electronic billboards and color supplements and celebrity endorsements were not the thing required.

Sandwiches were the thing, Ambrose said. Together with a place where one can rest, gaze up at a blue sky with a few gentle clouds, and take a breath. This place, Ambrose declared as he tapped his finger on the seat of a pew, is where the arses will go. Here is all the advertising you need.

A charming story, those who had heard it too often would say, but hardly believable.

Lunch, as promised, was improved. The waiter appeared with dipped madeleines. As madame prefers, he said. Zipper blushed at the discreet nods between her husband and the maître d' as Ambrose left the café. Nibbling at the chocolate, she watched her husband turn in the direction of the cathedral.

Zipper found a ladies' atelier and slipped into a new outfit of black blouse, red silk scarf, and white calf-length skirt. She remembered the restorative effects of French clothes. At a flower shop she bought a small bouquet of spring blooms. She walked down a steep cobbled lane and chose a quiet spot by the river with a clear view of the cathedral.

She opened her journal and thought of writing. *E is for Eiffel's tower, standing in Paris. L is for London and home. Z is for Zipper. T is for terrified. H is hopeless.*

The journal remained blank. Shadows lengthened as Zipper made her way up the lane to the cathedral. *L,* she thought, *is for lost.* The day's crowds had thinned and Ambrose was easy to find. He stood near the middle of the nave, at the center of a labyrinth inlaid in the stone floor seven hundred years earlier. A few pilgrims traced the labyrinth's penitent paths. Zipper was unnerved by how cold, how dark, how threatening the huge space was.

All around Ambrose were the cathedral's famous windows. Windows that poured blue light into the black and frigid Gothic space; that told stories and offered answers and provided comfort; that beckoned locals and pilgrims and tourists, the committed and the curious. And had been doing so long before television and billboards and supplements and celebrity.

Zipper hovered near the door, memorizing the view of her husband gazing around the cathedral while old women circled him on their knees. He spun this way and that, not knowing where to look next. He caught sight of Zipper and smiled.

Truly, thought Zipper. It had been one of his best days in advertising.

＝

Nearing midnight, the hum of Zipper Ashkenazi's mobile raised a sweat in the small of her back.

On the line: the publisher of the country's third-most-read fashion magazine. A sour-candy woman named Pru. A yeller in the workplace, a screamer on the phone.

WHERE ARE YOU?

The sound of Pru's voice turned Ambrose away from watching Normandy scroll past the train. He checked his watch and cringed sympathetically at his wife.

In France, replied Zipper.

THE ISSUE IS CLOSING. Photo needs another page. Your page? BLANK. "Fave Books of Fab People." Really, who bloody cares . . . WHERE?

I meant to call.

WORLDS ARE CRASHING, ZIP. Subs down. Ads canceled. Printer wants for payment. Have you resigned or something?

I should have called.

HOW BLOODY RIGHT YOU ARE.
I'm tired of keeping this rag afloat. Sick or
something?

I needed some time.

BE MY BLOODY GUEST. Meanwhile,
what am I supposed to do?

Give photo the page. I wish I'd called.
Honestly. Sorry.

NOT HALF AS BLOODY SORRY, Zip,
NOT HALF.

Something came up.

SOMETHING LIKE LEAVING? If you
jump, I bloody swear . . .

I need a month. Give or take.

NOW IS NOT the time. Ring when you get
back. THE BLOODY SEC—

Zipper closed the phone.

Ambrose borrowed his wife's phone and placed
a call to D&C. Someone would be there. Greta
was always there.

Grets? Ambrose.

France.

I know. Sorry.

Nothing. Something came up.

Sorry, no. I'm not leaving. Not exactly.

It's more personal. I'll explain later.

Yes, I should have called.

The client will be fine. Storyboards done, shoot booked, talent hired, wardrobe en route, print ads on my desk.

Yes, I'm sure. Wrote them myself.

The pitch? You do the pitch.

Can't. Sorry. It should be you anyway. It's your agency, your client. I'm just the help.

The client does not hate you.

He does *not* hate Germans.

Get the account lads to lend a hand. Threaten the sack. They'll understand that.

I'm okay. Thanks.

How long? A month. Maybe less. I'll let you know.

You'll do fine in the meantime.

I'll call if I can.

D

On their fourth day from home, Ambrose and Zipper sat in comfortable beach chairs watching the English Channel. It was a bright afternoon, the sun was high, the offshore breeze chilled a day more winter than spring. But for the time gone by and the time of year, they could have been any honeymooning couple.

Despite her squinting and her husband's pointing, Zipper could not see England. Just there, Ambrose kept insisting, jabbing his finger northward. Zipper could see the row of vacant bathing tents stretching along the beach, gaily striped for the coming season. A small girl in blue gum boots playing with a large dog at the water's edge, a calm sea beyond. A few working boats idled in the middle distance; a few heavy ships plowed the lanes farther out. But there was no far shore in her sight. Past the ships, said Ambrose. At the horizon. *Just there.*

Zipper gave up and lay back in her chair, annoyed. She knew the story. The Curious Talents of Ambrose Zephyr; or, The Business of Seeing Things Just There. To a disinterested listener, it might have been another tired story of the imaginings of children. To Zipper, it was a story a concerned parent might quietly slip to his new daughter-in-law, just before he and the missus waved their happy children off to a wedding weekend in Deauville.

According to Mr. Zephyr's story, at the age of eleven, perhaps twelve, Ambrose announced to his parents that he possessed a talent. The announcement occurred during the family's annual motoring holiday. They were on the Cornish coast.

I can see better than anything, young Ambrose said.

Any *one,* said his father.

Better than animals.

That is something, said his mother.

Better than binoculars.

You don't say, said Mr. Zephyr.

I do say.

And how did you come by this talent? asked Mrs. Zephyr.

Ambrose shrugged.

Indeed, said his father.

Ambrose's face began to glow.

He was standing on the last cliff of England, squinting as boys do, and seeing America. A soft blue lump, right at the horizon. Just there, Ambrose insisted, jabbing his finger westward. The Manhattan skyline emerged through the low ocean mist. His parents apologized for not being able to quite make out the details. They blamed the time of day and the angle of the sun.

Two summers later. On a tour through northern Europe Ambrose asked his mother to stop the car before each border crossing: could he walk the last few meters and stand on the frontier? At one such stop, recalled Mr. Zephyr, his son's left foot stood in Belgium, the right in Luxembourg. Ambrose then peered along the line (invisible to the senior Zephyrs) as it crossed the road.

On the same holiday Ambrose also announced he could see the difference between one country's soil and another's. The difference (and the talent to see it) was never defined. There was, young Ambrose said, just . . . something. Denmark was . . . browner, he offered his perplexed parents.

And the air too. From one country to the next, Ambrose could detect a change in the smell of things. Sometimes cleaner, sometimes mustier. France smelt like apples, Germany like freshly cut grass, Holland like wet socks. Ambrose declared he could smell it the moment he stepped over each border. Hopping in and out of Luxembourg, he explained: flowers . . . dogs . . . flowers . . . dogs . . . flowers . . . dogs.

As Zipper and her new in-laws stood on the platform waiting for the groom to return with the cross-Channel tickets, Mr. Zephyr's hushed story continued. His son's curious and increasingly annoying talent extended beyond the here and now. He could see the past. Events great and significant, faces grand and notorious, battles won and lost. The farther back in time the better, apparently. With the proper amount of squint, explained the boy, he could see what had happened or who had walked on the ground where he stood. Ten, a hundred, a thousand years ago.

Young Ambrose offered proof: the time he had emerged from the underground near the Tower of London and there was the Duke of Norfolk's piked and dripping head, as if the Virgin Queen herself had pruned it the day before. Or the summer he saw William the Conqueror wading through the sunbathers on the Hastings shore. Or the party of Druids he watched at Stonehenge while Mr. and Mrs. Zephyr read the visitor pamphlets. They were just a work crew, Ambrose assured his parents. Squaring a few lintel stones.

The end of the story came when Mr. Zephyr mentioned that he and the missus had once spent a lovely picnic afternoon watching their boy gaze across a flat and empty field in Flanders. He just stood there, said Mr. Zephyr. For hours. And I have no doubt, he added with a wink, the boy was in mud to his knees. Ah, here's your train.

Ambrose Zephyr gave up. Can't seem to see it either, he said. He lay back in his chair. After a moment or two of watching a few clouds pass overhead, he told his wife what he remembered.

The bloody queues. Bathing tents, ices, chairs, towels, the loo. Stretched the length of the beach. We changed in our room. Ran half naked through the lobby. It took us hours to find a vacant bit of sand. Nasty dogs and noisy children everywhere. The tents were a different color that year. Were they green? I remember it was too cold to swim. The Channel was rough.

First weekend of the season. Windy. Not even
the local boats were out. You hated the sand. Yes
you did. Insisted on wearing those horrible blue
trainers. From the ankle up you were
breathtaking. A fantastic bikini, red I think.
Fine, black. I drank too much calvados. You
read three books and mentioned what my father
had said on the platform. You asked—in that
voice you have—if I could see any soldiers on the
beach. I said very funny and told you they had
landed farther along the coast. Which made you
laugh . . .

Ambrose Zephyr's voice trailed off. A
moment later he spasmed himself awake.

Tired, he said, then drifted away again.

When she was certain her husband was well
asleep, Zipper walked along the Corniche. She
bought a postcard—an amateurish watercolor
from some time ago. The bathing tents depicted
were green, and judging by the crowds and the
queues in the painting, it appeared the
beginning of the season.

She returned along the water's edge. The girl
in the blue boots had coaxed her dog from the
water. Zipper watched them leave, then squinted
out to sea.

There was England. Just at the horizon.

E

The windy coast of . . . Zipper read, in a voice
she reserved for certain circumstances. They
were on a train bound for Paris, a flight to Pisa,
a short hop to . . .

Elba, said Ambrose.

Just a thought, said Zipper. Why not stay in
Paris? Get out of the airport for a while.

Napoleon wasn't keen on the place.

We could take a later flight.

But the views are spectacular.

They will be.

We'll be back to Paris in a few days, Ambrose
said. And we always go to Paris. You're not tired
of it?

Tired? Yes. Of Paris? No.

How's this then: *E is for Eiffel, a tower in Paris?*

Zipper pretended to frown. Not quite the
music of *The Windy Coast,* she said, but if you
don't mind.

Get out of the airport for a while.

Whatever you think.

It was a tone Ambrose could never resist. Nor had ever much tried to.

Zipper awoke in a modest room on the top floor of a hotel—their hotel—tucked in a corner of Place Saint-Sulpice. A band of sunlight found its way between the mismatched towers of the church across the square, through the window, and on over the bed. It came to rest across Zipper's face. She slid farther under the duvet, warm and safe.

Home, she thought. Another five minutes. Then she remembered where she was. Where Ambrose was. Off on his stroll.

Whether Ambrose remembered it or not was never the point. The fact remained: they *had* met, and it *was* the first time, on the Rue de Rosiers.

A younger Ambrose Zephyr is midway through his usual walk. Deep in the Marais, a spring downpour forces him into the doorway of an antiquarian bookshop. He huddles, his trench coat dripping on his shoes, and searches the sky for a break. He does not see the young woman coming through the door behind him.

A young Zipper Ashkenazi—on a break from

E

working a fashion shoot—purchases a second-edition *gastronomique* published many years before. The book is in only fair condition and she barters well. A good souvenir, she thinks, of a first trip to Paris. The small volume slips into her coat pocket and she opens the shop door.

Zipper does not see the young man's face as the bell above the door chimes an exit. Ambrose, fretting about his shoes, does not hear the bell.

In the politest French she can manage, Zipper asks the young man's back to excuse her. A startled Ambrose turns and stares at the young woman. Zipper waits, then begins opening her umbrella. Ambrose continues staring, oblivious to weather, shoes, umbrella.

The rain continues.

The staring becomes annoying.

After some time, Zipper breaks the young man's gaze and glances at his feet. Ambrose rediscovers his manners. He steps into the street and allows the woman by. He apologizes in the politest English he can manage. He would have removed his hat, had he owned one.

The rain pours and Ambrose stands watching the young woman disappear under her umbrella. As Zipper steps to avoid a puddle, she glances back at the young man and looks away.

He smiles, having caught her out. She
vanishes around a corner and chuckles at the
thought of the young Englishman's ruined shoes
and drowned hair. A hat, she thinks, might have
gone well with the trench and the weather.

Something had changed. The air seemed off.
The sunlight through the window felt cold.
Zipper thought it might be the cobwebs of a too
heavy sleep. She glanced at the bedside clock,
padded to the ensuite, and ran a bath. By now
her husband would be passing Notre-Dame,
stepping on the *point zéro* marker as he went.

His *flânerie,* Ambrose called it. It was habitual,
rarely altered in either route or duration.
Friends called it his cliché, mentioning the
beaten path, suggesting other sites and different
sounds. Ambrose would politely nod his head
and wander where he wanted. They have their
Paris, he would tell Zipper. I have mine.

She slipped inch by goose-bumped inch into the
steaming water. Her toes wiggled at the other
end of the tub. Zipper closed her eyes as the

heat went to her bones, releasing wave after raw wave of terror. She tried imagining something else, but all she could see was their time. Their Paris . . .

The narrow street off the Boulevard Saint-Germain with its family *boulangerie* and two-table cafés and produce stalls. Where they had always bought a workman's lunch and a bottle of *vin du pays*. Where Ambrose would sneak a foul cigarette while she selected a pâté . . .

The Bastille roundabout. Where he would narrow his gaze and point out peasants laying siege to the prison. Where she had mastered the grace of walking in heels amid the helter-skelter traffic . . .

Zipper's shoulders heaved, she gulped for air, fought for calm. She looked down at her body and thought of his hands.

In Place des Vosges. His hands on her. In the dark beneath Victor Hugo's window, her hands on him. Breathless mouths, wordless tongues, losing themselves. Under the plane trees in the middle of the night . . .

She buried her face in her hands. *You cannot have it,* she screamed through her fingers.

The antiquarian bookshop. Soon it would belong to other lovers, selfishly claimed as *their* Paris . . .

The *bouquinistes* near the Pont Neuf. He would be there . . .

Zipper pulled herself from the water, hurried to dress, ran for her life.

He would be there by now.

Zipper rushed along the quai toward the Pont Neuf, checked her watch. She was late. Yet she smiled. She knew where he'd be and it wasn't far away and she could slow down.

A *bouquiniste*'s stall caught her eye. It was decorated with the bric-a-brac of the printing trades: agate rulers, bindery clamps, typesetters' trays. A collection of old type blocks.

One particularly worn wooden cube felt soft and good in her hand.

Zipper found Ambrose at the downstream end of Île de la Cité. Lying on the cobbled breakwater that sloped at a comfortable angle into the Seine. He was, as usual, admiring the view along the river to the Eiffel Tower, peeking above the rooftops, far in the distance. Zipper sat beside him.

You smell like cigarettes, she said. How was the walk?

Ambrose lied. Lovely, he said. Zipper caught sight of his slowly trembling hands, the subtle curling and uncurling of fingers.

How was your lie-in? he said. Feel better?

Zipper lied.

As is the habit of lovers in Paris, they spent the rest of the day on the island in the Seine. They ate a workman's lunch, drank all the wine, waved to the *bateaux-mouches*.

At some point Ambrose lay his head in his wife's lap and stared through the trees to the sky. He said he thought it might rain. Zipper laughed.

Admit it, she said. It *was* you with the soggy shoes. Ambrose smiled.

What remained of the day passed quietly. Without a cloud in sight.

I bought you something, Zipper said. For missing Elba.

They were in a taxi en route to the airport. She put the wooden type block in his palm and closed his stiff fingers around it. No peeking, she said.

He knew the character by touch. Uppercase,

a bold sans serif from a headline tray. He felt
the sharp zig and zag of the letterform. The
smooth face of the block, the worn and rounded
edges. Feels large and heavy for something so
small, he said.

I bought you something too. Ambrose
handed her a fat and tired edition of *Les
Misérables*.

Zipper glanced through the rear window of
the taxi. A tower in Paris, tiny and far away,
flashed through the skyline and was gone. The
taxi merged onto the *périphérique*.

F

Late afternoon stretched across the Piazza della Signoria. A marble David—muscular, walleyed, tall for his age—ignored the sightseers crowded about his base. A few with cameras backed away from the horde, cautiously measuring their strides, trying to fit boy king and mugging companions in the viewfinder.

In a quiet corner of a café at the opposite end of the square, Ambrose Zephyr ordered wine. Two glasses. *Rapido,* he snapped.

Zipper was surprised at her husband's tone. She gave him a look he chose to ignore.

They sank low in their chairs. It had not been the day Ambrose had in mind. It had all been too much, too many.

Those who knew Ambrose would later say they were not much surprised by *F*. After all, they offered, hadn't his mother introduced him—*and*

at such a young age—to the great art of Florence?
Wasn't he proud—*annoyingly so*—of the university
away term he had spent flirting his way through
the city? Did he not know its architects, its
Medicis, its masters? By name *and* date, they said.

An old man moved past their table. He was a
picture of the casual Italian gentleman: polished
shoes, cufflinks and cravat, practical sunglasses.
He carried a walking stick, tapping it lightly on
the cobblestones as he moved along.

The stick missed Ambrose and Zipper's
table. There was a minor collision; a drop or
two of spilled wine, a stumble. The Italian
gentleman apologized as his hand searched for
the edge of the table. Ambrose swore under his
breath.

Zipper glared at her husband a second time,
applying more disgust, less surprise. Ambrose
slumped deeper into his chair and sulked at the
crowd across the piazza.

No harm done, Zipper said to the Italian
gentleman. He turned his body in the direction
of her voice and smiled.

Zipper found a third chair. The old
gentleman asked if he might rest. Just for a
moment . . . the joints, you see.

You smell like my wife, he said. Zipper was
embarrassed by her suddenly blushed cheeks.

When we would walk. In our evenings along

the river, she wore that fragrance. A wise and clever woman, my wife. This I know, she would say: A man can see a hundred women, lust for a thousand more, but it is one scent that will open his eyes and turn him to love. And he will never thank the angels for making him blow his nose that morning.

The sightseers under the marble boy king grew more boisterous.

These crowds, said the Italian gentleman. They take many photographs. Such a sad thing. Such a long way to come to take bad pictures of one's friends.

He shrugged. This city is too much for them, he said. Too many paintings, too many churches, too many Davids. Too many other people taking pictures. Can you see the duomo? someone will ask. I can see the back of your head, another will answer.

But enough, he blurted in Ambrose's direction. Life is too quick for such gloom. There are other things to see.

Ambrose scowled.

The old gentleman searched for Zipper's hand. Indulge me a bit of a game, he said. He took her hand and cupped it between his.

Signora's blouse, he announced after a moment, is as white as our marble. Crisp and tailored, like a man's. The cuffs are rolled, the collar is turned. Very casual. The buttons open just so and—forgive me, signora—there is perhaps a peek of black lace, a peek of something.

A smile inched across Ambrose's face. The gentleman continued.

She wears a silk scarf—reds and golds, I think. A flowing skirt, calf length. Red again, like Il Papa's cardinals. But it is late in the day—she has slid her sunglasses to the top of her head. A strand of hair hangs to the side of her face. She squints with the low sun. The feet of birds at the corners of her eyes. Have I missed anything?

Signora's shoes, offered Ambrose.

Aaaah, said the Italian gentleman, there you are. Now you wish to play my game. Very well.

They are . . . black. Yes. Flat. For too much rushing around. For too many people. For too much art. But I am guessing. Better, I think, for walking by the river?

Ambrose looked at his wife. Zipper noticed it was the first time his eyes had brightened all day.

A third glass was summoned and a toast to marble kings was drunk. Ambrose apologized for his behavior. Not my best day, he said. The Italian gentleman said there was no harm done. Ambrose asked him about his wife.

The old gentleman produced a small photograph and handed it to Ambrose. I have many, he said. They never seem to be where I leave them.

Ambrose smiled. He passed the photograph to Zipper.

She expected an old and faded portrait of a young and beautiful woman. Instead, the face that smiled stiffly from the photo was worn, fleshy, a little pale. But the eyes were clear, the hair well styled. An expensive scarf was tied loosely around the old woman's neck.

The face in the photograph had been embossed. Raised creases and furrows traced the features: scarf, hair, eyes. The shy smile.

I think she might be like your own signora, the Italian gentleman said. Something to see?

She was, said Ambrose. Is.

The Italian gentleman finished his wine and stood as best he could. He kissed Zipper's hand, begging forgiveness for leaving so abruptly.

I promised to meet someone by the river, he said, and tapped his walking stick across the piazza. As he passed the marble boy king, he pulled his pocket square with a flourish and quietly blew his nose.

The Mediterranean was passing far below them, Zipper Ashkenazi nudged her husband. You were talking, she said.

Sorry . . . dozed off . . . what? What did I say?

You kept asking why.

Why what?

I don't know. You were asleep.

Must have been dreaming.

Of?

A woman in the distance, approaching. She wades carefree through the desert sand.

She looks back toward the sun. She is barefoot, her sandals clutched by the heels, dangling in one hand. Her other hand holds the hem of her white cotton robe. Each step trails a fine stream of sand, caught in the hot wind and blown toward the Nile. The sun backlights her figure through the cotton, catches a glint of silver and ebony on her bracelets. Her walk in the desert has left her flushed and bronzed. Her hair is dark and fine.

A camel appears from nowhere, blocking the view. Everything swirls into the art on a package of cigarettes.

A boy lies on his bedroom floor. He is twelve, perhaps thirteen years old. He is drawing, with painstaking accuracy, the art from a pack of Camels. The arabesque curves of the serifs on the A. The ellipsed E. Three palm trees, two pyramids, one camel with its skinny legs. The pyramids tucked under the camel's sagging belly. The boy is careful, coloring the camel's visible eye a brilliant blue. He even includes the elegant ampersand between the words *Turkish* and *Domestic*.

The camel turns his head and grins.

Why so sad, Master Zephyr?

The boy frowns.

Death? Yes, yes, death hovers near us all. And it is sad that it makes us sad. But I know a story.

There once was a camel whose days begin in the shade of a palm on a nameless wadi, somewhere to the east of here. In the Sinai.

By the age of ten, the camel is a veteran of the trading routes from Alexandria to Tripoli. At twenty, he walks the rich Aswan run, kneeling politely as nervous Japanese women climb aboard to have their portraits taken. At thirty, he is done working, his knees worn thin. At forty, his days as a camel come to a peaceful end. Eyeing younger things in the Birqash market.

He is gutted and skinned. For seven days he feeds his owner, his owner's family, his owner's cousins, his owner's neighbors.

His hide is sold for a good and fair price in the bazaar to a maker of furniture who knows a good many buttocks would sit on such a fine and worthy leather.

Was there anything before his days as a camel, you ask? Yes, yes, Master Zephyr. The camel was a man. As you will be. Successful, well fed, loved by a clever and honest and beautiful woman. Happy they lived. Simply as husband and wife. Without extravagance, just off the high road between Suez and Aqaba.

The man misses his wife every day. Even now, as a camel in your drawing, as a comfortable chair under a large rump. But he sees her every day. He watches her sleep.

Why, you ask? There is no why, Master Zephyr. It is just a story. Life goes on. Death goes on. Love goes on. It is all as simple as that. Years from now, even you will return. Perhaps as the ocher that colors an artist's brush. Or a kindly stray cat in a small park in London. And you will love the birds you chase.

And then the camel winked, said Ambrose, and disappeared in a puff of sand.

Zipper blinked away a tear. He hadn't meant to make her cry.

G

The small bedouin woman sat on her haunches beneath the pyramids.

Her robes were black and billowed in the wind. She smoked a dark cigarette and played with a small Polaroid camera: holding it to the sunshine, tracing circles in front of her face, mimicking a self-photograph, watching for the soft image to emerge from its slot. She cooed and chirped and sang to herself. As a child might. Her grinning revealed the gaps of a few missing teeth.

She kept her place, apart from the mob of touts with their curative river water and stuffed crocodiles and plastic scarabs. Tourists scurried and counted out their dollars and pounds and yen and avoided her altogether.

Zipper noticed the woman, as Ambrose was otherwise occupied. He stood to the shade side of the cornerstone and leaned in to sight the edge of the Great Pyramid of Khufu. He closed his eyes to slits, gauging the angle of the corner, the smoothness of finishing stones, the tiny army of laborers far above. Naked and sweating and laying the final course.

Zipper left her husband and jostled away from the crowds. She found a quiet spot and sat in the hot sand. She watched the bedouin woman. Zipper wondered who or what was in the woman's photographs.

The woman stopped her play, beckoned Zipper. Come, come, she said. Sit, sit. There is nothing to be afraid of.

Ambrose leaned his face against the stone. He ran his hands across the rough surface, following a groove here, fingering a worn edge, clearing the grit from a notch there. Checking for true.

Hush, hush, said the woman.
Your singing is beautiful, Zipper said.
And you are afraid.
Zipper's heart thumped in her ears. She felt her hands go cold.

I should get back, she said. My husband . . .

I know what you see, the old woman said.
What frightens you. But what you see, you must
not fear.

Zipper's eyes welled up.

Everything will be well, the woman said. For
you. For your husband.

Zipper wiped her face and forced a smile.

The sign admonished visitors: To Climb or
Scale or Deface the Sacred Tombs Is Highly
Forbidden in Order to Protect Their Fragile
and Historical Nature.

Ambrose Zephyr likely thought otherwise.
Nothing so enormous and so immortal could
be that precarious.

Or that tempting.

Yes, yes. Hold his hand. He will not be away so
long. Not so long.

As she spoke, the bedouin woman turned to
watch a man struggling to climb the pyramid.

Zipper followed the woman's gaze to find her
husband standing on the cornerstone of the first
course of the Great Pyramid. Ambrose was
hunched over, hands braced on his knees,
wheezing and coughing.

The photograph is amateurish: the horizon tilting wildly, the subjects fuzzy and almost out of frame, a blurred black fingertip across one corner. In the photograph a man stands atop a great stone block, stiff and uncomfortable, beaming and posing as best he can. Like a schoolboy Lawrence, awkward but having gotten away with something.

He is pale in the dusky sun. His linen suit is scuffed and wrinkled and has become too large. Below him, a woman stands shy and reluctant. She is flushed, gently tanned, but appears lost.

H

Somewhere between the Giza plateau and Cairo
their taxi ran out of petrol. The subsequent bus
rattled and inched along with the city's traffic.
There were no seats and no handholds. There
was something that sounded like no brakes.

When Ambrose Zephyr and his wife arrived
at the airport, a sudden sandstorm had closed
the runways briefly but effectively.

Connections, and Haifa, were missed.

I

It would have been clear to those queuing for
the flight, had they noticed, that the
Englishman was having difficulty.

Ambrose Zephyr's face was drained white.
He smelled foul, soiled, rotten in his own sweat.
He stretched and curled and twisted his hands,
rubbed his joints, cringed when he stood,
shivered in the airport heat. Every few minutes
his eyes bulged in their dark sockets. Like those
of a person afraid of something he could hear or
smell but not see.

He snapped at his wife after she had asked
him, again, if there was anything she could do.

I am fine, Ambrose croaked.

Is there anything you need? Zipper forced
the question through her teeth.

I need to be left alone.

Zipper wanted to throw something at him.

Enough, he said.

Hit him.

Stop *fussing*, he said.

Stop him. Stop it. Go home.

Ambrose seemed to recover as the queue moved to board the flight to Istanbul.

They sat in the last row: Ambrose, Zipper, and an enormous young man who said that he was flying to visit his sister she is a nice dancer in a hotel viewing the Bosporus saving money for hospitality school so she may return to our family's taverna back home nice to meet you English couple on holiday I am presuming I study my English very much and you should come to our taverna someday such a nice couple you are though sir you do not look so well perhaps it is the flying maybe do you smell something? Where was I yes my sister the belly dancer she will help me and our father who is being most lonely since our mother left to be with her sister who is my aunt and raises many goats and makes their cheese best in all the Mediterranean yes now the card yes here it is the hotel where there is a view and my sister dances come if you are feeling well perhaps a *hamam* could help sir yes Turkish bath very good for all ailments can bring the dead back to life for madam as well I very highly recommend but remember please the hotel where my sister dances and sees the Bosporus if you get a chance my sister really is most good at the dancing perhaps a little heavy in the hips she should lose some weight but then who shouldn't ha ha there I think we are here and landed you nice English couple have a nice day it is a pleasure to be flying with you now remember you come and visit my family's taverna someday best coffee in all the Mediterranean truly even better than Istanbul perhaps we will see each other again remember a Turkish bath will do you no harm try the bath near the Blue Mosque very old very safe I know it well sorry let me slide over a little so you can get by apologies yes it is small in here I am perhaps too big for such a little airplane ha ha here let me move my so sorry can you get your leg over there okay sorry just a bit further maybe if I inhale a bit.

Walking to the taxi rank, Ambrose told Zipper that he had once imagined a view across the Bosporus. Or had seen it in a movie. He couldn't recall which.

Perhaps, said Zipper, a proper Turkish bath will clear your head. At the least the smell.

———

As boys of thirteen or fourteen are prone to do, Ambrose Zephyr received his first lesson regarding the intrigues of the Near East, and sex, from a woman.

The woman in question was not Polly or Penny or Patsy what was her name who had lived a few doors down. Prunella or Poppy or Priscilla was the gangly one. Breastless, with braces that cut his lip during a stolen kiss in his parents' garden.

No. The woman in question worked for the wrong side but longed to work for the right side. She was willing and well able to use her nakedness under clinging bedsheets. She was born on the steppes of Russia, nimble with a code machine and a gun, breasted, blond, and in possession of a suite overlooking the Bosporus.

Her name was Tatiana, said Ambrose as he and Zipper got out of the taxi in front of the oldest bathhouse in the city.

Of course it was, said Zipper.

And Bond meets her in the hotel room, said Ambrose.

The one with the view?

Right. She's wearing nothing but a silk ribbon around her neck. Completely naked, and our man in a dinner jacket. Imagine that.

Imagine that.

Zipper thought of a polite and curious boy of thirteen or fourteen years, sitting alone in a cinema. Possibly a matinee near Piccadilly Circus. His eyes bugging at the views of Istanbul.

Zipper emerged from the women's side of the baths to find her husband attempting to brush the wrinkles and smell from his suit. His hair was slicked flat to his head, his face was flushed and shaved, his smile was broad. A child freshly plucked from the Sunday tub. Zipper's expression was black, her face drained of everything but anger.

How was your bath? Ambrose asked.

Excruciating, said Zipper.

Large attendant?

Amazonian.

Small towel?

Humiliating.

Steam?

I've had enough.

Loofah glove?

You need to deal with this.

Massage?

That is not it.

Oil? Liniments? Palm fronds?
THAT IS NOT THE POINT.

Zipper stared at her husband in disbelief. They were still standing in front of the Velázquez Venus.

I mean yes, that is a point. Just not *the* point.

Sorry, said Ambrose.

Stop apologizing.

Sorry.

The point is you never say anything. I haven't a clue what you think about anything important.

Sorry.

Stop it. Stop being so damned . . . absent.

Ambrose shrugged.

Don't you care about anything? I mean really have an opinion. Beyond *it's lovely*?

Fine, said Ambrose. If you must know. I think the Velázquez is remarkable because it doesn't matter to me that she was an actress or that the sheets are black. I think abstract expressionism is crap. I think Brussels sprouts are crap. I think I could paint but I don't have the nerve. I think I am an unbelievably lucky man who is married to a woman who I think looks a little like the Rokeby Venus and I think if I open my mouth to say something I think is important I think she will discover she's married a fool.

You are many things, my love. A fool is not one of them. You're imagining things.

I am keeping things to myself. Having an opinion doesn't require sharing it with everybody.

It requires sharing it with me. Because *I* get to know what you think. *I* get to know you better than anyone else.

You do. Always have, always will, full stop. Let it go.

One more thing.

What?

You're wrong.

Am I?

Luck had nothing to do with us.

Outside the baths, Ambrose's scrubbed smile disappeared. THEN WHAT IS THE POINT? he said, smoothing another crease in his suit. Deal with what? What would you have me do?

CARE. Worry. Say something. Aren't you afraid?

Yes.

So?

So what? So there it is. Here I am. There's nothing to deal with. If there were, I would do it. But there isn't and I am terrified and this isn't happening to you.

You selfish, silent, shitty bastard. This is happening to me.

Really? In less than a month, you'll still be alive.

Really. I can hardly wait. Lying in on Sundays? At last. A decent cup of tea? Brilliant. No more squinting, no more visions, no more imagination, no more silence? I can hardly fucking wait.

In a lane near the Blue Mosque, around the corner from the oldest bathhouse in the city, curious pedestrians might have noticed a rumpled Englishman embracing a sobbing woman as if she might fly apart. She struggled to free herself, he held tighter. He whispered, she lashed out. He kissed her wet eyes, she turned her face away.

After a moment or two, the woman said she was fine. The Englishman handed her a thin bauble, a *boncuk.* He told her that Turkish mothers pin the blue glass trinket to their children's clothes. To keep them safe.

The curious might have watched for a few

more moments and then moved along and thought nothing more of it.

That evening Ambrose and Zipper found a bench in a corner of the gardens of Topkapi Palace, where grand and terrible sultans had once lived. Ambrose claimed the sultans had attended to the needs of their harems in this garden. After they had emerged from their baths, he said. Zipper said that sounded like something only a man would think up.

In the sultan's garden, Zipper and Ambrose stole as much love as they dared. A few buttons undone. Straps moved gently aside. The slip of a warm hand. The smell of bath oil and perfumed soap. Loofahed skin, sensitive to the touch. They whispered to each other not to worry.

The evening deepened and the lights on the Asian side grew more numerous. Zipper asked where the *boncuk* had come from. Ambrose said he had bought it while waiting for his lover to emerge from her bath.

They sat for a while longer and wondered whether the nice hotel dancer would ever get back to the taverna and whether she was as good as her brother had advertised.

In my opinion, said Ambrose, the best in all the Mediterranean.

The next morning near sunrise, London called nine times in as many minutes. None were answered.

Four calls came from Zipper's office, two from the offices of D&C. No messages left. One call just kept yelling *pick up, pick up, pick up, pick up.* One was from the Foreign Office: *In town. Drinks?* The ninth call left a message: *Sir's shirts are ready and may be picked up at his leisure as it were.*

Ambrose stood at the hotel window, looking at the Bosporus through the dawn haze. He wavered slightly, leaning his forehead against the pane to catch his balance. It was time to go home, Zipper announced, knowing her husband would never admit so on his own.

Ambrose turned and managed a sad smile.

Home then?

Home then.

They slept that night in their own bed in the narrow Victorian terrace in Kensington.

J, and the shirts, could wait.

K

Ambrose Zephyr stood shaving in his bathroom.

His wife hovered in the doorway, watching her husband's hands. A subtle tremor, more noticeable in the right. The razor hand. Ambrose leaned into the fogged mirror and pulled a slow stroke. His hands steadied. The knot in Zipper's stomach eased.

We can't keep avoiding them, Zipper said as her husband finished his neck and began on his chin.

I'd rather not be today's topic, said Ambrose.

Friends wouldn't do that.

Zipper stood beside her husband and rested her head against his shoulder. Ambrose looked at her reflection in the mirror. What he could make out appeared hollow. As if she weren't quite there.

Everyone does it, said Ambrose. One minute you are who you are. The next it's strange looks

and wringing hands and poor Ambrose is there
anything we can do Ambrose let's all dance on
eggshells Ambrose. Suddenly it's all that you
are. All you will be.

Ambrose held out his razor hand and
watched the tremor shake a few drops of water to
the floor. This, he said, is not me.

He looked back at the mirror. They, he said,
are not us.

When the Mankowitzes lived at twenty-six and
the Ashkenazis lived at thirty, the girls would
meet in front of twenty-eight. Neighbors said
that with *that pair*, that Katerina Mankowitz and
Zappora Ashkenazi, there was always much to
decide. What to do about boys. What to do about
Katerina's beastly little sister. What to do about
their hair, their shoes, their skin. Zappora
called her best friend Kitts.

When Kitts found a job as a photographer's
assistant, she put a word in with her employer
regarding a friend looking for work.

When Kitts thought she was pregnant,
Zappora found a discreet clinic. As it turned
out Kitts was late. The friends celebrated at
the local. Zappora bought a round for the house.

When Zipper announced she had met

someone, Kitts approved. As long as he can be trusted, she said. It was Kitts who found the wedding dress.

When Kitts left her most recent lover, Zipper made up the spare room. She used some of Kitts's photography to decorate. Kitts would never say as much, but what hung on the walls was worth thousands. Moody black-and-whites of back-lane characters in rough countries were much in demand by the world's collectors.

Pick up, pick up, pick up, pick up. PICK UP.

Zipper answered the phone.

Kitts said she was on her way.

Ambrose opened his front door and found Kitts glowering at him. She was, as always, tall and haggard. Like a woman just returned from working in a place with no running water. She called Ambrose a bastard and hugged him. Longer and warmer than usual.

Lovely to see you too, said Ambrose as Kitts went inside. He sat on his front step and lit a cigarette left over from Paris.

———

In her kitchen, through two pots of tea, Zipper came apart. She started laughing like a schoolgirl. L is for list, she said. W is for Was it something I did? D is for something I didn't do? S is for something I should have done?

She showed Kitts the journal, fanning the pages like a conjuror. She pulled odd items from the journal's envelope. Souvenirs, Zipper said. What a grand bloody tour it's been.

Other bits and baubles materialized from Zipper's pockets. Everything formed a small mound on the table.

A postcard featuring a muddy reproduction of an enormous Rembrandt.

A is for a portrait in Amsterdam, said Zipper.

A small and smooth stone, gray and warm. Barbaric Berlin.

A flattened lavender bloom, barely fragrant. Advertising in Chartres.

Another postcard, this time offering a jolly watercolored *Bienvenue à Deauville*.

A honeymoon by the sea, Zipper said.

A fat and worn copy of *Les Misérables,* an embossed photograph of an Italian woman in an elegant scarf, an unflattering Polaroid snap of Ambrose and Zipper by the pyramids. A child's blue glass bauble.

Our Paris, laughed Zipper. Florence, Giza, Istanbul. Did I mention we missed Haifa?

Zipper picked up the journal. Page after blank page.

And what will I have when he's gone? Nothing. No growing ancient together, no retiring to the *pied-à-terre*, no children, no grandchildren, come to that. No more. No life. Nothing. Blank.

But you never wanted children, Kitts said.

I never wanted *this*. I is for I don't know what to do.

Kitts sat in the eye of her friend's storm, nodded, shook her head, held tight, wiped Zipper's dripping face, put the kettle on, wept, buttressed, agreed. Listened.

When the worst had passed, Kitts did what she had done since the childhood meetings in front of twenty-eight. She said something smart at the precise moment when there was nothing to say.

He's right, the bastard. Live what's left. Live it as large as you both can. That's what he wants. That's what *you* want.

Zipper threw her journal on the table.

But the words. How do I start? Where do I end?

The words will come, said Kitts. They always do.

Wilkes and Zephyr met at university.

They took a loose interest in the other's academics: Ambrose sneaking his friend into a life-drawing class to prove that artists did not get erections; Freddie instructing his friend on the proper balance between single malts and thesis writing.

After graduating, they shared a shoebox flat in a hard part of London and lied on each other's CV. They began referring to each other by last name only. It sounded good, they'd explain. Something professionals might do.

When it appeared likely they were destined to drive cabs, Wilkes passed his foreign service examinations and Zephyr landed a junior position as a copywriter. Which, much later in their lives, they would characterize as ironic.

Between distant postings and demanding clientele, the friends rarely saw each other. They never reminisced when they did. They kept every piece of wish-you-were-here correspondence and look-what-I-created souvenir each had sent the other.

No one, least of all Zipper, could explain

why they had remained friends for so long and
at such distance. Or why they had even become
friends in the first place.

Drinks? always meant the Savoy bar.

All Ambrose would later say about his
evening with Freddie was how good it had been
to see an old friend. They spent the time talking
mostly of each other's work, said Ambrose. State
secrets, slagged clients, that sort of thing.

What likely occurred was that after enough
kirs and enough whiskeys, Ambrose reluctantly
described the circumstances. There would have
been long silences, pinched glances, calls for
same again please.

After some time the friends would have
found their Gallipoli courage and looked each
other in the face. There would have been tears
in their eyes. Stoic ones, but tears nonetheless.

Damn, Freddie likely said, turning away for a
moment.

Ambrose probably apologized.

The friends would have pulled themselves
together. Freddie, as always, would then have
said something clever and wise.

You need to edit. Enough with A through
Zed. Toss the list. You'll end up hating half the

places you go anyway. Think of Zipper. Stop dragging the woman about. Wasn't she the one who said it was time to come home?

At the end of the evening, the friends would have stood on the street waiting for taxis. They would have embraced, as old friends do when parting. If you need anything, Freddie no doubt said.

Right then.

Right.

Taxis would have appeared.

Neither friend would have said good-bye. They never had before.

J

Ambrose Zephyr would sometimes remark that a
better man was one supplied with an intelligent
woman, the ability to tango, and an able tailor.

For those who knew Ambrose, *an able tailor*
became the explanation for why Ambrose
Zephyr had stroked out Jaipur on his list and
penciled in Old Jewry.

Mr. Umtata sailed from home a younger man,
stowed away in the hold of a runt freighter.
When the authorities realized he was gone, he
wasn't missed. Good riddance, they said.
Another *kaffir* away.

On the day the freighter docked in London,
Germany was invading its neighbors. A week
later Mr. Umtata found work in the army.
Nothing at the sharp end of course, they said.
You understand. Still doing your bit as it were.

He learned a trade. Mind the break at the cuff, Major would say. A bit snug across the shoulder. Give those buttons a polish, there's a good fellow. Mr. Umtata's war raged through the officers' mess. When it ended, Major and his buttons went home to the country and Mr. Umtata went to Cheapside.

He took up piecework in a ladies' and gents' shop. Alterations to All Garments Our Specialty The Smartest Styles Within Bespoke Orders Upon Request Satisfaction Assured for All Closed Sundays. He enjoyed the ladies' work particularly.

He learned how to dance. To understand how the clothes move, he told his employer. Mr. Umtata was a small man whose teeth were too big for his mouth, but his partners did not mind. He was always impeccably dressed, he smelled heavenly, and he could move. Like Astaire himself, they said.

After twenty years Mr. Umtata purchased the shop. It was a narrow concern, too dark in summer, too hot in winter, and could neither boast nor hold the selection common among the Savile shops. But Mr. Umtata's handwork was slow and sure, his service humble, his discretion reliable. Observation and counsel were parceled out as he saw fit. Upon request.

They met the morning a younger Ambrose Zephyr produced his first television commercial: thirty seconds for the finest cleanser the mod seventies' housewife could ever wish to own.

The concept involved a red-haired actress, grinning in a mod seventies housewife manner, on her knees scrubbing the average English street—a tip to the product's mod seventies scouring power. What the woman's hot pants tipped to was left to interpretation. Old Jewry stood in as average street.

The commercial was to be filmed from an extreme angle, and Ambrose had split the seat out of his trousers checking the first setup of the day. An assistant from the agency shoved him through Umtata's door for repairs. The tailor's first advice: a proper fit through the buttocks.

When asked by Ambrose what he thought of the activity in the street, Mr. Umtata replied that it all appeared interesting but sir may want to reconsider the hot pants.

Ambrose became as regular a customer as wages and wear would allow. Jackets now and then, shirts by the gross, flirtations with bell-bottomed trousers (against contrary advice). At the rear of the shop, in a wooden box marked Active, Mr. Umtata kept a file card with particulars: *Zephyr, A. Dresses left, favors right shoulder, prefers contrasting linings. Poor color sense. Requires some direction. See also Ashkenazi, Z, (Mrs).* It was the only card filed under Z.

Ambrose brought Zipper to Old Jewry to meet Mr. Umtata, as a young suitor intent on impressing might. Do you approve? asked Ambrose.

Indeed, sir, said Mr. Umtata. I believe the expression is yin to your yang. And if I may be so bold, sir. Does the lady dance?

Mr. Umtata cut, lined, and hand stitched the suit Ambrose was married in—double-breasted, trousers in the full and classic style, startling yellow tie. At his final fitting, with Zipper observing, Ambrose suggested a matching yellow carnation for the lapel. Zipper rolled her eyes. Mr. Umtata frowned in silence.

I think it makes a statement, don't you? said Ambrose.

Indeed, sir, said Mr. Umtata.

Just the thing for the big day.

Quite.

Bit much?

As you say, sir.

Mr. Umtata also fit and altered Zipper's dress (an off-white vintage number, one

Zipper waited until the sun came through the front window, then made a cup of tea. She joined her husband on the front step.

I need to deal with the office, Ambrose said.

Zipper watched the neighborhood stray.

Loose ends, that sort of thing.

Zipper examined the dregs in her cup.

I should have called, she said.

Near Leicester Square stood the offices of Dravot, Carnehan. A few streets away stood the offices of the third-most-read fashion magazine in the country. Zipper and Ambrose had managed to work in the same part of the city, but neither one could remember when they had managed lunch together. Or ridden the underground as a couple off to work. Isn't it funny, thought Zipper, to be doing that now? They decided D&C would be first and best dealt with.

Few heads turned as Ambrose and Zipper walked through the creative department to his office. Everyone is too fresh, thought Zipper. Too busy. Too young.

Greta sat in Ambrose's chair, looking out the windows and fidgeting with his collection of type blocks. Without turning around she said how odd it all felt. D&C had gotten the account.

previous owner, purchased in Portobello Road). With my compliments, missus, Mr. Umtata said as he snipped the last thread and stood aside to allow Zipper a full look in the mirror.

The lady does indeed dance, said Zipper as she swished.

Mr. Umtata and Zipper then toasted her impending marriage with a deep and expert dip. To ensure proper movement, said Mr. Umtata through a toothy smile.

On the day, the newlyweds looked like famous people, despite the downpour in Kensington Gardens. Zipper's bouquet was a handful of small white rosebuds. Complemented by a small white rosebud in Ambrose's lapel. Mr. Umtata was unable to attend. Saturday was a brisk day at the shop in Old Jewry. He sent regrets.

Years later the wedding suit still fit. The linen number, however, was in urgent need to attention. And there was the matter of shirts being ready.

At the rear of the shop, Mr. Umtata uttered a stream of sighs. Ambrose asked if anything could be done. Zipper mentioned time was pressing. Mr. Umtata then suggested sir might strip to his boxers. Missus might want to take a seat.

In silence the tailor of Old Jewry worked his

needles and threads and scissors and irons. Ambrose searched for somewhere to put his hands. Zipper watched her husband's white skin, stretched thin over bone.

We've been abroad, said Ambrose.

Indeed, sir, said Mr. Umtata through the pins between his teeth.

Rather suddenly.

Indeed.

Traveled light.

So it would seem, sir.

Sorry for the rush.

As am I, sir, said Mr. Umtata, hiding the last seam, his eyes fixed on Zipper's wet eyes.

A fresh shirt was unwrapped. Ambrose strained out a smile as he dressed.

A miracle, Umtata. As always.

As you say, sir.

A bit loose across the shoulders though.

Indeed, sir. Shall we check the fit?

With that Mr. Umtata took Ambrose Zephyr in his arms. Allow me the lead sir, he whispered. The men dipped. Deeply, expertly.

Zipper Ashkenazi laughed out loud. For the first time in days.

L

The sun began to rise as Ambrose Zephyr sat on his front step. It was, still, his best time of the day.

He watched number twelve with his tiny dog. The elderly man frowned: he had forgotten his hat. Number eighteen, naked this morning and trusting that no one was awake at such an hour, gathered the morning paper from her doorstep. The neighborhood stray, ignored, eyed the birds in the park across the way.

The night fog burned off. For Zipper Ashkenazi, standing at her front window wearing one of her husband's new shirts, it looked to be a rare morning. A fine one, for the time of year.

Ambrose sipped his coffee, certain his wife was catching just five minutes more. He waved to number eighteen and sheepishly smiled an apology for having seen more than he should have. The elderly man went home to get his hat.

—

I'll just clear up a few things, said Ambrose.

More annoying than odd, said Greta.

I won't be long.

Big meeting next week. Strategy.

Most of it you can toss.

Tactics. New staff.

The plants are fake. They'll last.

Global campaign. Much work to do.

Just a few things.

The billing will be huge . . .

Greta's voice trailed out through the window.

Ambrose picked over his desk. A photograph of himself at a location shoot: longer hair, horrid bell-bottomed trousers, a red-haired actress nearby. A newspaper style manual. A pocket atlas, leather-bound with ribbon marker. A few travel brochures from the sixties: *Ski Zermatt This Year, Beautiful St. Moritz, Now Is the Time for Geneva.* A moody black-and-white photograph of Zipper. Taken in a rough country in a younger time.

You can keep the type, said Ambrose. My gift.

Greta turned away from the window. Tears flowed down her cheeks and dripped from her chin.

Bloody annoying, she said.

Yes, it is, said Ambrose.

I hate this. I want to go home.

I hear Berlin is lovely this time of year.

Ambrose smiled and kissed Greta warmly on both cheeks. He pocketed the photograph of Zipper and left.

Pru was yelling at Milan or Paris or New York or her assistant when Zipper appeared at her door. Pru threw her earpiece across the room, glanced at Ambrose as if he weren't there, and began yelling at Zipper.

I quit, said Zipper. Her life had unraveled. It didn't need Pru picking at the threads. She wished *quit* had come out sounding angrier.

YOU WILL NEVER write again, Pru said as quietly as her disposition could manage. I WILL SEE TO IT.

Perhaps you will, said Zipper.

MNOPQRSTU

It took most of the day for Ambrose and Zipper to reach Hyde Park. Here and there Ambrose's gait had slowed to the shuffle of an old man. Crowded pavements and clogged traffic had taken their own toll.

Through Kensington Gardens the pace improved. In other times, on better strolls, Ambrose would say he could see the King out for his morning ride: mounted on a dapple gray, overdressed in lace and buckles, the court blundering behind him like a bad comedy sketch.

They stopped to rest at the edge of the Round Pond. Canvas deck chairs had been put out for the season. Ambrose looked across the water and the swans and into nothing.

What would you have done? Zipper asked.

———

I would have sat on a beach in Mumbai, said
Ambrose, and had my hair cut. For extra rupees
the barber would have told my fortune. *Sahib will
be leading a surprising life.* You would have worn a
sari the color of aubergine.

New York. I'd been there once. On
business? No. You were there. For the spring
shows. Did you take me along? Or was it
business? Funny how I can't recall. It was much
farther away than I remembered.

O. O . . . is Osaka. I bow to the department
store hostesses; they cover their smiles when they
hear my Japanese. You and I are at the theater.
Bunraku, I think they call it here. A tragic tale.
Montagues and Capulets, judging by the acting.
You cry during the final act. P. Pago Pago.
Paddington. Perth? I learn a new language,
Queensland gone walkabout. We waltzed, didn't
we? The beach . . .

There was an odd half smile on Ambrose's face.
He looked away.

Keep going, said Zipper. Please keep going.

What?

R. You were about to say R.

———

. . . Rio . . . the beach. Ipanema. They have professional foot washers, imagine that I can see Africa from the beach, and you are not so young or tall but very tanned and quite lovely and there's Shanghai sea of tai chi women scowling at me, a tiny string ensemble of five-year-olds playing something in a minor Barber's *Adagio*, sad for such little hands . . .

Don't stop, said Zipper.

I can't.

T?

Can't remember. Timbuktu?

Don't worry. U then.

Ambrose looked at his wife as if he didn't know her. The King, he said, is not much of a horseman.

Oh God.

Ambrose and Zipper did not move until dark. The panic was slow to ease.

The moon rose above the treetops, and they walked the rest of the way home. As they turned into their road, Ambrose said he remembered.

V

We were staying in a *pensione* near the Piazza San Marco. I woke up too early. It was difficult putting on the linen number in the dark, but I didn't want to wake you. I borrowed a blanket from the hotel and walked across the piazza.

Everything was mist and fog. It was raining, softly, off and on. The air felt cold for the time of year. It was too early for the cafés to open.

I found a chair and pulled it to a better spot near the lagoon. The gondolas were still tied to their posts, bobbing like toy boats. I wrapped myself in the blanket and soaked in the hazy view across the lagoon. In all the years we talked about Venice and pictured Venice and dreamed of Venice, did we ever once imagine it might smell?

I was sleeping when you found me. You said you had worried. I'm fine, I said. How could I not be? I've kept a promise.

You smiled and said yes, finally, I had.

The waiters were unstacking chairs, wiping tables, opening umbrellas. The piazza began filling with tourists bundled against the chill, griping about the weather, trying to fit the campanile in the viewfinder.

You and I left the edge of the lagoon and went off in search of breakfast. We found the Bridge of Sighs, lost our way to the Erberia, and decided we weren't hungry anyway. We were wet and cold and our clothes reeked of dead fish and it couldn't have mattered less.

Zipper said that was how she remembered it as well.

Z

I'll be along in a minute, Ambrose said. Zipper
went upstairs and crawled on top of the duvet.
She stared at the ceiling.

What felt like hours later Ambrose appeared
at the bedroom door. Zipper helped him into
bed, wrapped him in an extra blanket to stop the
shivering, curled herself around him. She was
drifting in and out of sleep when the air in the
Victorian terrace turned suddenly thick. The
silence startled her awake.

Zipper cried quietly for a long while before
ringing Kitts and Freddie. They would know
what to do, whom to call.

She kissed her husband's eyes and went
downstairs.

———

On the kitchen table she found her well-thumbed edition of *Wuthering Heights,* a ragged slip of paper tucked in the first few pages. *Chapter One. 1801—I have just returned from a visit . . .*

On the paper, Zanzibar had been scribbled over. In the margin was written *Zipper.* With the proper amount of swoosh to the Z, and in a remarkably steady hand.

———

A few evenings later, Zipper Ashkenazi sat on
her doorstep under a threatening sky. She wore
a borrowed linen jacket, too large across the
shoulders, but warm enough against a stiff
spring breeze. Beside her stood the leather
suitcase from under the bed.

She watched number twelve carry his tiny dog
around the park. Number eighteen hurried
along the pavement, a few minutes behind her
time. The neighborhood stray strolled toward
the birds.

When the elderly man passed by, he paused.
He put down the dog and turning smartly
toward Zipper, took off his hat and bowed. The
dog stood unsettled at his master's feet, trying to
ignore the neighborhood stray. The man
replaced his hat, collected his dog, and walked
slowly home.

Number eighteen kept walking past her

waiting children and stopped a step or two below Zipper. The woman's smile was shy. After a moment she found something to say. She told Zipper that she had always enjoyed her column in the fashion magazine. It was the first thing she read every month. You always have an interesting story to tell, she said.

There was another pause. Yes, well, the woman said finally. Tea, she suggested, might be nice. Perhaps . . . sometime . . . when you're ready then.

Zipper thanked the woman for her kindness. Tea would be brilliant. Soon. The woman's children waved their art, and off she went.

Zipper sat for a while longer, watching the empty park. It began to rain. She opened the journal that had come from the bookshop in Amsterdam. With slow and gentle care, Zipper emptied the contents of the envelope into Ambrose's suitcase. From a pocket of her jacket she pulled a type block. Boldface, sans serif. She paused, then put the worn wooden cube back where it belonged.

She turned to the journal's first page, wiped her hand down its blank face, thought for a moment, and began to write.

This story is unlikely.

ACKNOWLEDGMENTS

Martha Kanya-Forstner, Christine Pride.
   Suzanne Brandreth, Dean Cooke.
   Maya Mavjee, Kristin Cochrane, Bill Thomas.
   Martha Schwartz, Judith Stagnitto Abbate.
   Kelly Hill. Hannah Richardson,
   Sanger Richardson.

Rebecca Richardson. Without whom the above would
have never read a word. Nor applied their expertise,
grace, and generosity to the matter at hand.

CSR 12.06

READERS' GUIDE

≡

1. The book opens with an epigraph by Elizabeth Bishop, excerpted from her poem "Questions of Travel." Why is it significant?

2. CS Richardson has called this book "a fable, a parable on the notions of love and loss and relationships, and how far you would go in the name of love." How does the tone of fable impact the way you read this book?

3. The descriptions of Ambrose and Zipper are parallel in structure, with paragraphs devoted to their tastes in clothing, music, literature, and food, and brief descriptions of their appearances and personalities. Why do you think Richardson chose to describe them in this way? Do you see other symmetries in the structure of this novel?

4. What lessons does Ambrose carry with him from the life, and death, of his father?

5. Ambrose is dying from an illness that is cloaked in mystery in every aspect save its fatality. Why do you think Richardson chose to leave the illness unnamed and vague?

6. A camel utters with equanimity some advice in Ambrose's dream: "Why, you ask? There is no why, Master Zephyr . . . Life goes on. Death goes on. Love goes on. It is all as simple as that." Discuss Ambrose's dream. What does it reveal about the state of his mind and heart?

7. In chapter "Z," why did Ambrose leave the list in Zipper's book? Why that book? What is the gift of his message?

8. At the novel's close, Zipper opens her notebook and writes, "This story is unlikely," repeating the phrase that opens the novel. Why do you think Richardson chose to loop the book's narrative in this way? Did it change your perspective on the preceding pages?